Brain Gains

Brain Gains

So, You Want to Be Your Child's Learning Coach?

DAVID P. SORTINO

ROWMAN & LITTLEFIELD
Lanham • Boulder • New York • London

Published by Rowman & Littlefield
An imprint of The Rowman & Littlefield Publishing Group, Inc.
4501 Forbes Boulevard, Suite 200, Lanham, Maryland 20706
www.rowman.com

6 Tinworth Street, London SE11 5AL, United Kingdom

Copyright © 2020 by David P. Sortino

All rights reserved. No part of this book may be reproduced in any form or by any electronic or mechanical means, including information storage and retrieval systems, without written permission from the publisher, except by a reviewer who may quote passages in a review.

British Library Cataloguing in Publication Information Available

Library of Congress Cataloging-in-Publication Data

ISBN 9781475831856 (cloth : alk. paper)
ISBN 9781475831863 (pbk. : alk. paper)
ISBN 9781475831870 (electronic)

Contents

Author's Note		vii
Acknowledgments		ix
Introduction		xi
1	The Exterior Brain	1
2	The Interior Brain	7
3	Organization and Time Management	15
4	Windows of Opportunity	33
5	Listening Intelligence	41
6	Memory	53
7	Reading	71
8	Learning Styles	83
9	Test-Taking	99
10	Left/Right-Brain Teaching	111
Appendix		123
Bibliography		133
Index		141
About the Author		

Author's Note

DEAR READER

Brain Gains: So, You Want to Be Your Child's Learning Coach? represents the final link to my first two books of the *Brain Smart Trilogy*. This third book recognizes the challenges children face each day in learning environments defined by *mandated curriculums, mandated testing,* and *shortened school years.* For example, from kindergarten through high school, your child will be responsible for assimilating and accommodating different school curriculums, regardless that these mandated curriculums often do not take into account the variations in the cognitive and emotional levels of each student.

Problems can develop for those children who are not academically at the curriculum's grade level due to additional multiple challenges and distractions, such as adapting to the peer group, family dynamics or disharmony (divorce, child abuse, etc.), and delayed physiological/social development and/or cognitive delays, all of which could cause a lifetime of learning difficulties.

Finally, a major strength of this book is the offering to parents and teachers the opportunity to incorporate learning techniques used by myself and other successful learning coaches and/or learning specialists that readers can employ for specific student learning challenges.

Most importantly, parents and teachers will not only have hands-on learning techniques and strategies they can employ as learning coaches, but their students and/or children will also receive knowledge catered to their specific learning needs that they can use for future learning challenges.

David P. Sortino, Ed.M., Ph.D., June 2019

Acknowledgments

- Ms. Jan Corbett
- Dr. Thomas Lichona
- Mr. Tom Horner
- Dr. Dagmar Hoheneck-Smith
- My family: Jennifer, Abby, Shai, and "Henry the Pug"
  and
- The parents, teachers, and children who helped bring the Brain Gains Approach to completion.

Introduction

Brain Gains begins with the chapter "The Exterior Brain," which details the multiple brain areas that are required to work together for a successful learning experience. For example, Dr. David Sousa, noted learning specialist and author, describes the complex reading process as such: "Let's say reading begins with *d-o-g*. Next, the visual signals travel to the visual cortex located in the occipital lobe of the brain. The word 'dog' signals are decoded in an area of the left side of the brain called the angular gyrus, which separates it into basic sounds, or phonemes.

"The entire process activates the language brain areas located in the left hemisphere near and in the temporal lobe, where auditory processing occurs. The auditory processing system sounds out the phonemes in the head as in *duh-awh-guh*. Finally, Bronca's and Werneck's areas supply information about the word from their mental dictionaries, and the frontal lobe integrates all the information to improve meaning—'a furry animal that barks'" (Sousa, 2005).

The school schedule and/or curriculum can also produce "multiple learning challenges" to your child's learning brain. For instance, the first 20 minutes of each school day is an impactful learning time. However, we need to understand the importance of this open period and why teachers *should not* waste this critical period of the school day on such mundane tasks as taking attendance, lunch count, and so on. Studies describe this impact as the "primacy-recency effect," or the conundrum that the brain remembers best what comes *first and last* and retains less of what is in the *middle*.

Therefore, it would make sense that teachers begin the school day by connecting the day's most important information to the previous day's lessons, a practice that has shown to activate higher learning with their students. (Note to reader: This procedure is also referred to as the anticipatory set.)

Additionally, the primacy-recency effect would support the last 20 minutes as a critical time, as well. It is for this reason that teachers should consider reviewing the school day's last 20 minutes with students to support the primacy-recency effect. You can test this concept by asking your students or children what they remembered from the previous school day.

The follow-up chapter to the exterior brain is "The Interior Brain," with an emphasis on understanding the nuances about how to optimize your student's learning potential. In other words, the emotional connections in our mid-brain or limbic system often determine the level of your child's "learning interest."

For example, the interior brain's limbic system's or thalamus determines if the learning experience *is positive or negative*. If positive, the thalamus sends an impulse to the hippocampus for bonding, memory consolidation, and higher-order thinking. If threatening, the impulse is sent to the amygdala, and the reaction is a fight-or-flight response, and memory consolidation and intelligence can be short-circuited. This entire response may take only a matter of *seconds*, but such experiences can last a lifetime and actually be a threat to future learning experiences.

We move from the internal and external areas of the learning brain to the more demonstrative with chapter 3, "Organization and Time Management," which addresses some of the most serious learning challenges to your student's learning potential. Common complaints by teachers and parents range from, "he's completely disorganized . . . all over the map," "he rarely does his homework, and at the same time . . . puts off assignments to the last minute," "spends way too much time on his computer or phone!" and so on.

Swiss developmental psychologist Jean Piaget (1896–1981) recognized the lack of organization with children's brains in his early studies connecting learning to cognitive development. Piaget emphasized that our bodies are organized systemically or interactively, developmentally, and structurally. In other words, Piaget's research emphasized that the brain does not operate in a vacuum, separate from the body, but it instead takes a systems approach and views the brain and body as a *whole*.

My previous reading example illustrates the fact that for the brain to function effectively, *all systems* need to work as one. Apply this concept to a child's developing brain and we understand why good organizational and time management skills are essential for an organized and focused learning brain; the way your student learns this valuable *Brain Gains* technique is to create a hands-on, organized weekly schedule and require they know their schedule by heart as well as the importance of sticking to it!

Sticking to a schedule should begin with "visually/spatially" checking their schedule at the beginning and ending of each day. When students develop the habit of visually/spatially connecting with their daily/weekly schedule, they are stimulating areas of the brain that connects with the hippocampus, the part of the inner brain associated with bonding. For example, when they see the words "mathematics test," they do not just see the words, but their brain should process all aspects of what could go on with the upcoming math test, including emotional responses of fear as well as confidence.

Further, they may think of academic areas that need restudying or even a positive sense of what they know. In short, tuning in to their so-called visual/spatial intelligence can open up a whole new learning experience that can facilitate higher-order learning.

Along with connecting with the weekly school schedule are additional organizational techniques, such as employing a "monthly calendar" advertising the most important dates and activities, including adding notable school achievements such as "GREAT JOB ON YOUR MATH TEST!", "I WILL COMPLETE ALL MY SCHOOL ASSIGNMENTS BY THE END OF THE WEEK!", "THINK POSITIVE THOUGHTS!", and "SUCCESS IS 90 PERCENT PERSPIRATION AND 10 PERCENT INSPIRATION!" You get my point.

Again, when we tune in to positive "visual icons," we are also tuning in to our brain's emotional limbic system or hippocampus, which can lead to bonding and positive thoughts about your student's learning experience.

The chapter titled "Memory" follows, and it describes various aspects of specific memory types that your student will need to use for optimal learning. For instance, the "declarative" or "explicit" memory types are defined by oral communication (school lectures and social interaction) to the "episodic" (autobiographical and/or family interaction) and "semantic" (the world of words, facts, and language). The bottom line is this: All students (aka, learning coaches) need to have a firm understanding of the different "memory types" they will need to employ in school, particularly how memory connects with higher-order learning.

Once more, an important fact about memory and learning begins with your student's school schedule and the primacy-recency effect, or why students remember the first and last segments of the school day, lessons, and conversations, and usually forget the middle. Therefore, students need to be aware of such memory lapses by holding fast throughout the entire lecture. Simply being aware of how your brain works and when it is most vulnerable and not falling prey to the primacy-recency effect is a good place to start.

Another example of the effect the school schedule can have on your student's memory is the "block schedule" used by some secondary schools. For example, within your normal 80-minute block period, students could be more focused if teachers include short breaks throughout the 80-minute block schedule. Studies show that after every 20 minutes, students could lose 10 percent of attending behavior or memory. At the end of an 80-minute lesson, students could lose about 30 minutes of actual attending behavior. Therefore, take short breaks to counteract the discrepancy in attending behavior (Sousa 2006).

Finally, this can also be applied to homework or study periods. (Note to reader: Please see the Appendix section "The Pyramid of Learning" for research detailing students' highest and lowest retention rates after 24 hours.)

The chapter "Listening and Intelligence" is another critical chapter that should be taught in early childhood and continue throughout adolescence. This is because listening skills are associated with the adolescent's need for an "identity," which is often accentuated by a certain lack of listening when they reject family values for the values of friends.

One major school listening challenge is students who tune-out class lectures due to boredom or simply due to their brains' inability to "sequence" conversations or class lectures. Studies show that "elementary school children who play video games for more than two hours a day are 67 percent more likely than their peers who play less to have greater-than-average attention problems" (Klein 2018).

Additional listening challenges could be due to the adult's level or tone in speaking to the child or student. To be exact, when girls are spoken to in a high-pitched voice, they perceive it as a threat; for boys, it is the opposite. Moreover, boys' listening skills actually increase if the teacher is more animated and mobile during the lecture, while girls are more responsive when the teacher is more stationary.

The most opportune times when your child's brain and body is most receptive to learning a skill is described in the chapter "Windows of Opportunity." For example, from ages three to 10, children's brains and bodies ("kinesthetic intelligence") are more receptive to music instruction, which is why the Suzuki Method of training has shown to be most successful with musical training because the child learns to "intuit" music by complementing the sensory-motor areas of the child's brain.

Often discussed but rarely connected to the child's learning brain is "emotional control," or what to expect emotionally from children at various developmental stages. From around six months to about three years is when emotional control is often most challenging. During this period, the child is fiercely egocentric and focuses solely on getting their needs met. When their needs are not met, parents or caregivers will often resort to overgeneralization and labeling such children as with the "terrible two's."

However, upon further analysis, the terrible two's is nothing more than the child's immature brain overtaking his rational brain. In short, I recommend an excellent book written by Dr. Thomas Lickona called *Raising Good Children* (Bantam Books 1984), which describes what to expect at each stage of development from early childhood to adolescence.

The chapter called "Learning Styles" describes why readers need to learn *Dr. Richard Felder's Learning Styles Theory* because it could give you a heads-up on how certain types of learners function best in the classroom as well as support or a multisensory approach to teaching and curriculum development. A multisensory approach to teaching and curriculum development occurs when lessons are designed to meet the needs of *all* learners. That is, students whose learning preferences are more kinesthetic (physical) or verbal (linguistic). Readers are also encouraged to research the work of Dr. Howard Gardner and his theory of multiple intelligence.

For example, two of Felder's "eight learning styles" are called "active" and "reflective." Specifically, active learners often have difficulties sitting at a desk before they are literally hanging over its sides or simply standing at their desks during a learning experience. If you have such a child, he or she is in good company with famous writers such as Nobel Laureate Ernest Hemingway, who wrote his novels standing up at his fireplace mantle, and Henry Wadsworth Longfellow, who wrote his famous poems standing at his desk!

Additional techniques to support the "active" learner would be for such children to sit on swivel chairs to allow freedom of movement. Also, creating an elevated desk that allows the active learner to stand rather than sit can help such children's bodies to deal with the need for movement as well as to stimulate their kinesthetic intelligence.

In my opinion, the general purpose of taking a learning-style position is that it could lower negative perceptions of learning and increase a positive paradigm of potential learning and to support a multisensory learning concept. Still, we need to respect all learning styles—the active learner's bodily needs or the reflective learner's need to reflect and process information. With support and knowledge of different learning styles, the parent or teacher could see greater learning and intelligence with all students regardless of ability or temperament.

As you discovered in my opening paragraph, reading, which is the focus of chapter seven, represents one of the most difficult and important educational challenges students could face because it affects all aspects of classroom learning. In truth, if a student is not reading proficiently by third grade, they could struggle throughout most of their school experience, both academically and psychologically (Annie E. Casey Foundation, 2010).

"Further, children who were read to as newborns displayed a larger vocabulary, as well as more advanced mathematical skills, than other kids their age. There is also a direct link between how many words a baby hears each day and their language skills. Another study found that babies whose parents were more verbally engaging scored higher on standardized tests when they reached age three than children whose parents weren't as verbal" (Diproperzio, n.d.).

Successful reading programs that have shown to improve student's reading proficiency and comprehension are "Echo reading," "Choral reading," the "Shared Reading Program," and "Reading Theatre."

Lastly, there are those children who display serious reading problems, such as "developmental dyslexia," who are being helped by remediation programs such as Fast-forward, developed by Scientific Learning Associates, a group that has given support to both teachers and parents to help readers of all ages, levels, and disabilities remediate reading deficits.

The chapter "Test Taking" describes why some students are poor test takers and what they can do to improve their test-taking skills. The first step is for students to learn the nuances of the most popular types of tests, such as true/false, multiple-choice, and essay.

For example, the multiple-choice format is commonly used in testing because the exams are relatively easy to grade, and the questions effectively evaluate students' knowledge of facts and understanding of concepts.

Unlike multiple-choice tests, with true-false tests, answers should not be changed unless one is absolutely sure of the answer. If one is not sure, it is best to stick with the original impulse and write an explanation in the margin of the test.

Also, students will learn how they can lower test anxiety by tapping in to their kinesthetic intelligence or the physical aspects of test anxiety. Studies show that students can combat test anxiety and improve performance by writing about their worries immediately before the exam begins, according to a University of Chicago study published in the journal *Science* (Harms, 2011). Also, simply consuming certain foods can change one's test-taking abilities, such as eating dried fruit (fructose = dates, mangoes, etc.) and maintaining adequate hydration (water) before the test, which has shown to increase a student's test scores.

Our final chapter, called "Left/Right-Brain Teaching," is an excellent chapter to add to teachers' and parents' repertoire to support the *Brain Gains and/or Learning Coach* concept.

For example, due to mandated curriculums, mandated testing, and shortened school years, teachers are being asked to support school curriculums that represent a purely left-brain approach to teaching. In other words, many school curriculums focus almost entirely on the left side or linear, sequential, analytical thinking and ignore the right side, which supports a spatial, holistic, and abstract learning approach. Although we use both sides of our brains with day-to-day challenges, there are certain differences between both sides of our brain or how our learning brain can affect groups of learners whose brains specialize in "right-brain learning."

I begin this last chapter with a personal "multisensory" teaching lesson and how I changed a special school's traditional curriculum content to support both brain sides of learning handicap and severely emotionally disturbed students ages 14 to 19. In short, I integrated our school's curriculum with a driver's education lesson by having our students plot car routes from Connecticut to California. To achieve this goal, the students would need to use mathematics to find the shortest distance from Connecticut to California as well as compute the costs for gasoline, hotels, food, and so on to successfully complete their cross-country trip.

In addition, the students would need to research (study skills) and write (English/writing) about the history of the cities as well as the different geographic formations (science) they would experience on their trip to California.

The entire lesson would take about six weeks, and as a final requirement for all students, a presentation of their projects was given at a parents/teacher night. From the students' perspective, "It was the best school experience we ever had because you taught us something we could use in real life!"

To conclude this chapter, I identify various schools (Montessori, Steiner, etc.) and/or curriculums that apply left- and right-brain learning as a philosophy as well as offer readers a left/right-brain assessment to identify the differences between the left/right brains of their students.

Brain Gains: So You Want to Become Your Child's Learning Coach? represents techniques I have used during my 40 years as a learning specialist and/or learning coach with students of all ages. In addition, the information readers can take from this book could prove invaluable to parents and teachers in support of the *learning coach concept.*

As a side note, I also recommend to readers my first two books: *Brain Smart Trilogy: A Guide to How Children Learn: Understanding the Brain from Infancy to Young Adulthood* (Rowman & Littlefield Publishers, 2017) and *Brian Changers: The Most Important Contributions to the Advancement of Children's Learning and Intelligence* (Rowman & Littlefield Publishers, 2019). These will further your knowledge as a learning coach.

Good luck,
David P. Sortino, PhD, June 2019

1

The Exterior Brain

> But when you're in front of an audience and you make them laugh at a new idea, you're guiding the whole being for the moment. No one is ever more him/herself than when they really laugh. Their defenses are down. It's very Zen-like, that moment. They are completely open, completely themselves when that message hits the brain and the laugh begins. That's when new ideas can be implanted. If a new idea slips in at that moment, it has a chance to grow.
>
> —*George Carlin*, Brainy Quote, *2018*

THE EXTERIOR BRAIN

The frontal lobe represents the rational and/or executive center of our exterior brain in charge of higher-order thinking, learning, and judgment. The frontal lobe is still undeveloped at adolescence (emotions are difficult to control), which is why most adolescents have problems with impulsive behavior and good decision-making. Equally important, the frontal lobe is responsible for working memory, decision-making, organization, problem-solving, and planning (Goldberg, 2001).

If you truly want your child to be a successful learner, then feed the frontal lobe. Parents can start by making their child's life *organized* and *predictable*. Today's students are often faced with a great deal of disequilibrium through no fault of their own. Divorce, separation, different parenting styles, developmental delays, electronics, and so on all affect a child's organizational intelligence, which is located in the frontal lobe.

For instance, excessive exposure to electronics ("screen time") has been shown to seriously affect the frontal lobe, the seat of executive thinking. According to Dr. Victoria Dunckley, author of *Reset Your Child's Brain* (2015), "Excessive screen time appears to impair brain structure and function. Much of the damage occurs in the brain's frontal lobe, which undergoes massive changes from puberty until the mid-twenties. Frontal lobe development, in turn, largely determines success in every area of life—from sense of well-being to academic or career success to relationship skills."

Brain Gains #1

If you want to be more successful in all aspects of life, you need to protect and take care of your brain—and the brains of those you love, especially your kids, because their brains aren't fully developed until about age 25. This is when the prefrontal cortex (PFC), the part of the brain that controls decision-making, judgment, forethought, focus, and impulse control, among other functions, is considered fully developed. For this reason, it is so important that you help your children protect their brains—so they can mature into healthy and productive adults (Amen, 2018).

Brains Gains #1a

Please Google *Dr. David Sortino: Teen Athletes and Performance-Enhancing Drugs.*

The temporal lobe is responsible for sound, music, and facial recognition, as well as our brain's major speech centers (i.e., the left brain). To stimulate this part of the child's brain, parents can play music to young infants and encourage music lessons for the obvious reason that the temporal lobe is a major area of auditory intelligence.

Brain Gains #2

"The Mozart Effect": fact or fiction? Does listening to Mozart increase a child's intelligence, particularly when played to infants? My opinion is that good music is like good food, so it makes sense to feed the temporal lobe areas of the child's brain.

The occipital lobe is located in the posterior of the brain and responsible for visual processing and spatial intelligence. The jury is still out that hanging a black-and-white-lined mobile over the infant's crib works well to stimulate this area of the infant's brain. Also, studies by Gaser and Schlaug (2003) have shown that brain scans of nine- to 11-year-old children have revealed that children who play musical instruments have developed significantly more grey matter (i.e., neurons) volume in both the sensorimotor cortex and the occipital lobes. In short, *increased grey matter may account for superior performance on language tasks.*

Brain Gains #3
Parents can support optimal early vision development naturally by interacting with their babies and playing with books and toys. All of these activities stimulate a baby's visual growth (Urban Child Institute, 2011). For additional information, please see section #4 in the Appendix, "Toys, Games, and Activities," for your child's vision from infancy to seven years old.

Brain Gains #4
Jigsaw puzzles are an excellent strategy to stimulate your child's visual skills or occipital lobe.

The parietal lobe is located at the top of the brain and deals with spatial orientation, calculations, and some types of recognition. Be sure to allow your child the space to explore his home environment as soon as he can crawl, since it feeds into the parietal lobe as well as the cerebellum and his kinesthetic intelligence (i.e., touch).

Brain Gains #5
"Opening a door, combing your hair, and placing your lips and tongue in the proper position to speak all involve the parietal lobes. These lobes are also important for understanding spatial orientation and for proper navigation. Being able to identify the position, location, and movement of the body and its parts is an important function of the parietal lobe" (Bailey, 2019).

The "motor/soma-sensory cortex" lies between the parietal lobes and frontal lobes (executive thinking). The somatosensory cortex is also responsible for the coordination of sensory data representing various parts of our body. In addition, a strip (two bands: motor cortex and somatosensory cortex) at the top of our brain between the parietal lobes and frontal lobes works with the cerebellum to coordinate motor skill development and learning (Sousa, 2006). The reason why cursive writing is so important to the motor/somasensory cortex is that it develops the hand-eye coordination necessary for the development of this area of the brain.

Brain Gains #6

The work of Iris Hatfield, creator of the New American Cursive Penmanship Program, believes in the connection between cursive writing and brain development as a powerful tool to stimulate intelligence and language fluency as well as improved neural connections in the brain. She explains, "The physiological movement of writing cursive letters helps build pathways in the brain while improving mental effectiveness. And this increased effectiveness may continue throughout the child's academic career" (2018).

Brain Gains #7

Please Google *Dr. David Sortino: Intelligence and the Lost Art of Cursive Writing.*

Moreover, this part of the brain, like the cerebellum, is affected by the sense of touch, which is why *breast-feeding* is so important to brain development and the bonding process. Parents need to explore the work of Maria Montessori and Rudolf Steiner and how kinesthetic learning promotes *bonding* through physical stimulation, especially for boys. (Please see *Magical Child* by Joseph Chilton Pearce [Bantam Books, 1986], *The Absorbent Mind* by Maria Montessori [Holt and Company, 1986], and *Understanding Waldorf Education: An Introduction for Parents* by Jack Petrash [Floris Books, 2009].)

Brain Gains #8

Grey matter, located on the surface of the brain, is thickest in girls at 11 and in boys at 12 years of age. It then shrinks while white matter grows in formation with learning (National Geographic, 2016).

Brain Gains #9

Please Google *Dr. David Sortino: When Boys Get More Attention Than Girls*.

Brain Gains #9a

The brain's grey matter represents a massive number of tiny computers and white matter the dense wiring (Research Gate, 2014).

2

The Interior Brain

I would not put a thief in my mouth to steal my brains.

—*William Shakespeare,* Othello

THE LIMBIC SYSTEM

The limbic system involves your child's emotions and motivations, especially those associated with survival. The major systems involved with the limbic system as related to your child's learning are the thalamus, the amygdala, and the hippocampus, all of which are connected to memory consolidation and higher-order thinking. For example, damage to the hippocampus may result in an inability to form new memories, which is essential for a successful learning brain. Further, students who have problems with taking tests or athletes who "choke" during active competition could be suffering the consequences of stress to the limbic system's amygdala due to fear of failure!

Brain Gains #10

Please Google *Dr. David Sortino: And Remember, It's Only a Test!*

Brain Gains #11

"Because the limbic system is the mediator between thought and feeling, it is easy to see why emotion is so crucial to making good decisions and thinking clearly. Emotions can disrupt thinking and learning. When we are happy, we have a 'clear mind,' but when we are upset, we can't 'think straight.' Positive emotions such as joy, contentment, acceptance, trust, and satisfaction can enhance learning. Conversely, prolonged emotional distress can cripple our ability to learn. We all know how hard it is to learn or remember something when we are anxious or depressed" (Lawson, 2002).

The thalamus, often called "the decider," plays a major role in deciphering incoming sensory information. If incoming information is threatening, the thalamus sends the information to the amygdala, and this part of the brain goes into a "fight-or-flight mode" (it takes about eight seconds), causing memory consolidation to become short term.

On the other hand, if the information is nonthreatening, it is sent to the hippocampus, where short-term memory is converted into long-term memory. It is for this reason that most learning experiences should be directed to all the intelligences or multimodalities. (Note: Please Google *Steiner, Montessori schools*, etc.)

Brain Gains #12

"The hippocampus, a structure involved in memory, usually is larger in women; the amygdala, a structure involved in emotional processing, is larger in men. It is also true that the cortical mantle (made of grey matter) is thicker in women, and women tend to have a higher ratio of grey matter to white matter (white matter being the kind of brain cells that are insulated)" (Jarrett, 2012).

For example, when you match the child's multiple intelligence (linguistic, mathematical, visual, kinesthetic, intrapersonal, interpersonal, naturalist) with creative teaching styles, you are sending a message to the thalamus, which signals the hippocampus that learning can be a positive ("bonding") experience. Hence, the child who has a positive attitude or confidence toward learning will also have greater memory consolidation that can carry over to higher learning and potential school success.

Brain Gains #13

"A switchboard operator is responsible for receiving information, interpreting the information, and making the proper connections to send and receive information. In the brain, the thalamus serves like a switchboard operator for the body. The thalamus is critical in relaying sensory information to the brain" (Arrington, n.d.).

Therefore, the first teacher you select for your child should be an *expert* in early childhood education because new learning paradigms could be developmentally challenging or inappropriate for some children's limbic systems and/or learning brains.

Brain Gains #14

One of the greatest detriments to your child's learning potential and intelligence are school environments that do not support the multiple intelligences (Gardner, 1983).

Unfortunately, many of today's schools are attached to mandated curriculums and mandated testing, which forces teachers to concentrate almost entirely on "left-brain learning," or the linear, logical, and mathematical intelligences, despite the fact that many students also exhibit learning strengths in the visual or kinesthetic intelligences. The end result is that those children whose brains are wired for other intelligences could develop a perception that they are "not school smart" and consequently could spend a lifetime struggling to learn.

Brain Gains #15

Neuroscientists once believed that the mature brain was incapable of producing new neurons—that is, the neurons you had at birth, or shortly afterward, were the ones you would have for your entire life. However, research suggests the opposite. New neurons have been found in the hippocampus, the region that is critical in the formation and storage of new memories. University College London neuroscientist Eleanor Maguire discovered an enlarged hippocampus in the brains of London cabdrivers.

Cabbies spend two to four years memorizing London's intricate streets grids. Maguire found that cabbies' right posterior hippocampus, the region devoted to spatial navigation, were 7 percent larger than the norm. Neuroplasticity shaped the cabbies' brains as they learned more and more about how to navigate London's streets (Jabr, 2011).

The cerebrum is the largest area of the brain, representing almost *80 percent* of the brain's weight, and it controls and integrates motor, sensory, and higher mental functions, such as thought, reason, emotion, and memory.

Thus, the cerebrum is empowered by multimodality curriculums or, again, affected by "multiple intelligence."

The cerebellum is located below the cerebrum and encompasses about 11 percent of the brain's weight and contains more neurons than the rest of the brain put together! Whether one is a slam-dunk basketball player or the track star completing a triple jump, we need to thank the cerebellum for its ability to coordinate our bodily functions.

Also, the cerebellum allows for finer movement, such as thoughts, sense, touch, and memories. Studies have shown that the cerebellum is engaged and differentially activates in response to phonologic and semantic tasks such as decoding new words. These results indicate that the cerebellum contributes to the cognitive processes integral to reading as well as to dyslexia (Fulbright, 1999).

Brain Gains #16

Teachers and parents need to be particularly observant of primary-age children's fine motor skills as a reflection of the cerebellum's development and its effect on reading.

Brain Gains #17

Please Google *Dr. David Sortino: The Writing Is on the Wall!*

Again, what makes the cerebellum so extraordinary is its role in the development of sports and muscle memory. (It is every great athlete's wish to obtain a high degree of muscle memory.) Ice skating is a good example of the gift of muscle memory as bodily movements become automatic. Professional figure skaters must concentrate on the choreography of the routine as well as on their ice-skating skills, so a healthy cerebellum is essential.

Brain Gains #18

Please Google *Dr. David Sortino: Neurofeedback: How to Get into the Zone?*

The brain stem ("reptilian brain") is concerned with our physical safety, signaling watchfulness for danger when necessary. It also tells us if we should move to a "fight-or-flight" response. The reptilian brain saves us from the car that runs the red light by causing us to look before we cross, even though we have the right of way. The rational brain cannot function that quickly. When we think of survival, we need to thank the reptilian brain!

Brain Gains #19

Next time you take your child to the beach, watch how your child will lie down on the warm sand and stretch out like a lizard sunning on a rock. This could be the reptilian brain beckoning.

BRAIN CELLS (85 TO 100 BILLION AND COUNTING)

The billions of neurons that occupy our brain have tens of thousands of branches, which are called dendrites. Dendrites are finger-like nerves that take in information from other nerve cells.

Brain Gains #20

Notice the large, leafless trees that cover a winter landscape? A dendrite looks much like a leafless tree.

Between the dendrites are "synapses/gaps" where electrical signals are sent out to other nerve cells through neuronal transmitters, which are fueled by the chemical dopamine. Dopamine is a neurotransmitter that helps control the brain's "reward" and "pleasure" centers.

Brain Gains #21

Please Google *Dr. David Sortino: Electronics and Your Child's Novelty Seeking Brain.*

Dopamine also helps regulate movement and emotional responses, enabling us not only to *see* rewards but also to *experience* rewards. The synapses transmit information from one nerve cell to another. The more quality experiences your child has, the more interconnections are created. Researchers suggest that your child's earliest learning experiences ("episodic memory") should always begin with touch to stimulate the cerebellum or his kinesthetic intelligence, which fosters greater bonding ("sense of touch").

Brain Gains #22

"'There is already substantial literature looking at the positive effects of touch in infants,' including links between touch and an infant's growth and emotional development, says [Annett] Schirmer, a psychologist at the National University of Singapore. 'Our work adds by showing a relation specifically to the social brain . . . and extending this to an older age group, suggesting that benefits exist beyond infancy'" (Gholipour, 2016).

TAURINE

This important chemical is found in breast milk and has high amounts of amino acids, which feed the development of the child's brain. The true positive about your child's brain is that it will continue to develop brain cells throughout his entire life. The cliché of "if you don't use it, you lose it" can be traced to our sensory neurons that do not regenerate, and that is probably why we have so many—about 100 billion. Finally, many scientists believe that the only nerve cells that do regenerate are located in the hippocampus.

Brain Gains #23

"Taurine, an amino acid thought to help with neurological development, is found in breast milk, especially the early secretions known as 'colostrum.' Research shows that taurine is especially essential in the first few weeks of an infant's life. Whether you feed your baby breast milk or formula, there are ways to ensure your child gets ample amounts of taurine in his diet" (Barnes, 2017).

Colostrum is the first stage of breast *milk*. It is also much thicker than the *milk* that is produced later in breastfeeding. *Colostrum* is high in protein, fat-soluble vitamins, minerals, and immunoglobulins. Immunoglobulins are antibodies that pass from the mother to the baby and provide passive immunity for the baby (American Pregnancy Association, 2019).

Moreover, brain scientists stress that we must be proactive about stimulating your child's brain with activities, such as puzzles, brainteasers, and, of course, the arts, particularly music, which stimulates the brain's auditory centers.

Brain Gains #24

Why did piano keyboard training improve spatial reasoning performance by 34 percent, while computer keyboard training did not? It could be due to the combination of tactile input from striking the keys, auditory input from the sounds of the notes, and the visual information of where one's hand is on the keyboard. Also, this information supports the suggestion that children tap their feet and sing to learn their math facts (Sousa, 2005).

Another important fact about the brain and the if-you-don't-use-it-you-lose-it cliché is called "proliferation" and "pruning." We have more brain cells as babies than at any other time in our life. Pruning occurs when the nobs on the brain cells die off. This begins in the first few months of life. Brain cells that do not find a job to perform are most apparent between the ages of six to 25.

Between ages six to 12, "gray matter," or dendrites, thickens, which explains brain weight gain. Some scientists believe that attention deficit hyperactivity disorder (ADHD) occurs during this period because there is a proliferation of brain cells, causing the brain to become overloaded (i.e., stressed). Recent theories about the high incidence of ADHD could be due to the lack of gray matter, which is more densely packed.

Brain Gains #25

Between the ages of 12 to 25, gray matter decreases, white matter increases, and the myelin sheathe (i.e., insulation around the new cells) thickens, creating a high level of learning and intelligence. The thickening of the myelin sheath can also work against your student, particularly for adolescent males. That is, the struggle of most adolescents is the challenge of dealing with a maturing body with all the desires of adults, while also being attached to an emotional brain that is not fully developed, causing irrational judgments and impulsive behavior (Sousa, 2005).

In addition, because the amygdala is larger in adolescent males than in adolescent females, their impulsive behavior and weak judgment appear even more extreme. Fortunately for girls, the hippocampus is larger—the seat of relationships ("bonding") and memory consolidation, which may be why girls are more interested in boys at an earlier age.

BRAIN FUEL

A poor diet is every parent's challenge for his child's learning brain and intelligence. Oxygen and glucose (i.e., sugar) are essential sources of fuel for the brain. The greater the learning challenge, the greater the need for fuel! Low amounts of oxygen (i.e., lack of exercise, or nature-deficit disorder) and glucose (i.e., food) in the blood can produce a tired child/student, especially during adolescence. A good nutritional breakfast is the key.

Brain Gains #26

Please Google *National Guidelines for Children and Adolescents 2013*.

Smoothies with protein powder are a quick fix for the student who is perpetually late or tardy in the morning and/or for the student who can quickly drink his favorite smoothie while running out the door. Also, water is needed to move one neuronal signal to another. Low consumption of water reduces neuronal signals. Finally, water keeps the lungs moist to allow for the efficient transfer of oxygen into the bloodstream. Place a small thermos of water in your student's backpack at night (one eight-ounce glass of water per 25 pounds per child).

Brain Gains #27

Studies show that there is an increased percentage in cognitive performance (i.e., test-taking) with long-term memory (35 percent) and working memory (21 percent) when young adults were given a mixture of 50 grams of glucose and an eight-ounce glass of water 30 minutes prior to test-taking (Macrae, 2012).

CRITICAL PERIODS

Pregnant women should be aware of their diet and/or food intake. For example, alcohol consumption (fetal alcohol syndrome [FAS] has been shown to be a factor with children who exhibit attention deficit disorder [ADD] and ADHD). In addition, medications, smoking, and so on during this period of accelerated brain growth increases the risk not only of addiction but also of mental defects, as well as learning disabilities, including inattention, poor memory, hyperactivity, weak problem-solving skills, immature social behavior, lack of emotional control, poor impulse control, and poor judgment.

Brain Gains #28

"Researchers studying more than a million children in Sweden have found that babies who are born prematurely have an increased risk of developing ADHD as compared with their full-term siblings" (Goodman, 2011).

3

Organization and Time Management

TIME
Each day it opens a new account for you.
  Each night it burns the remains of the day.
  If you fail to use the day's deposits, the loss is yours.
  There is no going back.
  There is no drawing against the tomorrow.
  You must live in the present on today's deposits.
  Invest it so as to get from it the utmost in health, happiness, and success.
  The clock is running. Make the most of today.
  To realize the value of ONE YEAR, ask a student who failed a grade.
  To realize the value of ONE MONTH, ask a mother who gave birth to a premature baby.
  To realize the value of ONE WEEK, ask the editor of a weekly newspaper.
  To realize the value of ONE HOUR, ask the lovers who are waiting to meet.
  To realize the value of ONE MINUTE, ask a person who missed the train.
  To realize the value of ONE SECOND, ask a person who just avoided an accident.
  To realize the value of ONE MILLISECOND, ask the person who won a silver medal in the Olympics.
  Treasure every moment that you have, and treasure it more because you shared it with someone special—special enough to spend time with you. Remember that time waits for no one. Yesterday is history. Tomorrow is a mystery. Today is a gift. That's why it's called the present!

—*Anonymous*

Organizational and/or time management skills represent a major ingredient for building a successful learning brain. Our bodies, our brains, and our world are organized into systems; even the word *organization* contains the root word *organ*.

Renowned Swiss developmental psychologist Jean Piaget (1900–1981) recognized the importance of organization, adaption, and learning early in his career. He theorized that the mind and body do not operate independently from one another and that learning is, in general, subject to the same laws as all biological activity.

Piaget emphasized that our bodies are organized systemically, such as the digestive system, circulatory system, and so on. Apply this concept to a child's developing learning brain and we begin to understand why good organizational and time management skills are essential to an organized and focused learning brain and *why* it is essential that your student creates a hands-on organized weekly schedule and sticks to it!

For most species to survive, they need to be organized to adapt to changing environments. In our case, such environments are the school classroom or homework study time. For example, each year, your child will be faced with an entirely new curriculum spaced out over a finite number of days. Include mandated curriculums and testing and you begin to understand the learning conundrum for some children to keep up with the school curriculum.

In addition to such learning challenges are the different student cognitive stages that can seriously challenge a child's ability to learn but also the child's perception of their learning ability. Studies show that within every classroom are often multiple student cognitive stages that can affect a teacher's ability to teach or reach all students (Kohlberg, 1973).

It is for this reason why parents and teachers need to possess the learning tools to address the impact of multiple classroom stages, mandated school curriculums, and mandated testing as well as the many disruptions in a student's life that can affect learning.

One strategy is to hire a learning specialist or coach in learning techniques to address disruptions, and the other is to employ this book's information and become your child's personal learning coach.

Bottom line: You cannot assume that teachers are able to meet the learning needs of all children, which is why some children fail to reach grade level. Ultimately, through years of trying to catch up to the school curriculum, some children become so frustrated with the learning process that they drop out of school or simply underachieve.

In my opinion, children who fall behind in the primary grades begin the drop out cycle, and each year they struggle and fall further behind.

Also, a reoccurring problem many children face is that their actual learning skills often begin with disorganization in their lives, particularly in the home. To be exact, the home environment and the development of organizational skills are crucial to higher-order learning. One reason we are seeing certain children fail to learn and use their innate learning potential is due to the disorganization and distractions present in their personal lives.

Sadly, for some children, their early years don't necessarily have to begin this way if the parents or guardians consciously realize the importance of the infant's emotional needs are directly linked to organization, adaption, and the child's developing brain. In other words, from the moment the child steps onto the world stage, the child instinctively attempts to organize the family environment through "cries for attention" to their bodily needs. The child will cry when one of these essential needs is not met: food, comfort, love, sleep, and so on. In short, the child's brain is simply communicating its need for a responsive organization to survive.

As the child grows older, you will find many children who are simply trying to adapt to the disorganized lives of their parents. This can include separation, divorce, blended families (three days with one parent, and three days with the other), and pressure on single parents who must work and parents who are two-wage earners. In short, this endless list can affect a child's learning foundation and potential ability for years to come.

As a result, we are creating a learning brain that is poorly trained to adapt to other organized learning environments such as the "classroom learning model." Teachers instinctively know the importance of organizational skills by structuring classroom lessons and/or learning environments that are highly organized to support learning that is systemic or interactive, structural, and developmental. In fact, the school "system" and all schools, in general, must *be systemic* to truly be successful. Again, the incidence of student failure begins early with in-home environments that do not prepare children for future learning organized environments (i.e., schools), which can be traced to the disorganization in their personal lives.

Therefore, the next time you hear an infant cry, it is only his way of telling us why organization is directly connected to adaptation and survival.

STRATEGY #1: CREATE A DAILY SCHEDULE

The first assignment I ask of new clients is to create and adhere to a daily/weekly block schedule. For their second visit, I ask the student to recite from memory their weekly schedule. More often than not, recitation of their weekly schedule is difficult because schedules can change from week to week due to the unpredictable and busy lifestyles of today's students.

However, after a few weeks adhering to their weekly schedule, the student learns quickly how much more predictable the world becomes when they experience the feeling of an organized brain. In time, the student actually begins to demand organization and predictability from parents.

(Note to the reader: The creation of a weekly schedule works well for grades three through high school. For younger students, parents should try and create a more flexible schedule that is more visual or includes pictorial images they can paste on or next to the various scheduled time slots.)

Follow these directions: Ask your student to list their daily schedule for an average day. Be sure they include electronic time, chores, homework, dinner, sports, playtime, sleep, extra help, school activities, and so on.

7:00 AM	2:30 PM
7:30 AM	3:00 PM
8:00 AM	3:30 PM
8:30 AM	4:00 PM
9:00 AM	4:30 PM
9:30 AM	5:00 PM
10:00 AM	5:30 PM
10:30 AM	6:00 PM
11:00 AM	6:30 PM
11:30 AM	7:00 PM
12:00 PM	7:30 PM
12:30 PM	8:00 PM
1:00 PM	8:30 PM
1:30 PM	9:00 PM
2:00 PM	9:30 PM

Now that your student has listed activities onto their 30-minute block schedule, they should have greater awareness as to how they sequence their time during an average school week. Further, another reason for the creation of an effective schedule is finding out times when your student is most or least focused. By creating a "structured and predictable" schedule representing an average school day, you are connecting the student's brain to specific times and activities such as waking up, dressing, eating breakfast, brushing their teeth, going to school, returning home, doing homework, and so on. All these systemic transitions should be organized and reinforced into their learning brains to reinforce higher cognition levels.

Brain Gains #29

"The part of the brain we use to predict the immediate future has been identified by Jeffrey Zacks, a cognitive neuroscientist at Washington University in St. Louis, Missouri. He carried out functional magnetic resonance imaging (fMRI) brain scans on volunteers watching film clips of everyday scenes. The participants showed increased activity in the midbrain dopamine system (MDS) just before and after a scene changed, indicating this brain area is involved in both anticipating and responding to events" (Gupta, 2011).

Once we teach the student to be aware of the rhythms of their habitual daily behavior, they can then begin to apply this understanding of their behaviors to school or learning situations, such as his school schedule. "At 9:15 a.m., I am ready for math; at 10:15 a.m., I am ready for language arts and reading," and so on.

In addition to what is being habituated, there is also a great deal of learning that is not defined. Educators often refer to this undefined learning as the "hidden curriculum."

Brain Gains #30

"The hidden curriculum concept is based on the recognition that students absorb lessons in school that may or may not be part of the formal course of study—for example, how they should interact with peers, teachers, and other adults; how they should perceive different races, groups, or classes of people; or what ideas and behaviors are considered acceptable or unacceptable.

"The hidden curriculum is described as 'hidden' because it is usually unacknowledged or unexamined by students, educators, and the wider community.

And because the values and lessons reinforced by the hidden curriculum are often the accepted status quo, it may be assumed that these *hidden* practices and messages don't need to change—even if they are contributing to undesirable behaviors and results, whether it's bullying, conflicts, or low-graduation and college-enrollment rates" (Glossary of Education Reform, 2015).

In addition, creating a defined weekly schedule can help define your student's highest and lowest learning periods. For instance, some students are more focused in the morning, while other students are more focused in the afternoon as well as in the evening.

Brain Gains #31

"Most of us spend every minute of our waking hours occupied either doing or thinking about the things on our to-do list. This disequilibrium within our day-to-day schedule is a common source of discontent, but science suggests a busy brain can actually benefit our mental health. A recent study published in the journal *Frontiers in Aging Neuroscience* found adults with a packed daily schedule fare better in brain health, specifically cognitive function, than their less busy peers" (Women's Brain Health Initiative, 2016).

STRATEGY #2: COLOR-CODE YOUR STUDENT'S DAILY SCHEDULE

Step 1: Your student should identify the blocks of time when he is most alert or focused. He can color his highest interest level in blue. Next, identify time blocks when his interest level is medium or in between, and color that orange. Finally, mark the time blocks when he is least focused or tired the color red.

Step 2: Just before bedtime, he should reexamine his most-focused time periods of the day and think why he was more focused and interested. He should follow the same routine for areas that are colored orange and red or ask why he was least focused during these time blocks. For instance, if his worse time is in the morning, he might need a better breakfast, or perhaps he might need to get up earlier.

Step 3: Once he defines his highest- and lowest-focused time periods, especially for middle/high school/college students, he should reexamine strategies to improve his weakest focusing periods of the school day. For example, he might meet with his school counselor about scheduling his easiest and/or most-difficult classes during the periods of the day representing the high, medium, and low colors. Also, if he is not a morning person, he could schedule PE, art, or electives for the first period. The same should hold true for afternoon classes.

Brain Gains #31a

"Adolescent sleep patterns have been surveyed by investigators in many countries from virtually every continent around the world, and a consistent finding is that the timing of bedtime on school nights gets later across the middle school and high school years (roughly ages 11 through 17 years). Rise times on school mornings, by contrast, tend to stay relatively consistent except in countries such as the United States, where the starting time of school moves to an earlier hour at the transition to high school. Weekend sleep for teenagers tends to delay further, and the difference in the amount of sleep reported for school days versus weekends becomes more pronounced as children pass into higher grades (i.e., greater reported sleep on weeknights than school nights)" (Carskadon, 2011).

Researchers believe that monthly calendars advertising long-range planning for special activities can stimulate the higher centers of your child's brain (i.e., prefrontal cortex), when you connect the present to future events and activities.

STRATEGY #3: BUY A LARGE MONTHLY CALENDAR AND WHITEBOARD

Place his monthly calendar in the most visible activity area of the house, including one in your student's bedroom. The monthly calendar should be one of your most important strategies for the creation of an organized brain. The monthly wall calendar should list all monthly activities, including school activities, tests, sporting events, important dates, and so on. In addition, the monthly calendar will be a good reference for family meetings on Sunday nights before the school week so that all family members can discuss important upcoming weekly activities.

Brain Gains #32

Please Google *Dr. David Sortino: Contracts, Adolescence, and Family Values.*

In addition, the whiteboard allows your student to write important activities, notations, or simple praises such as: "I WILL GET AN 'A' ON MY SPELLING TEST THIS FRIDAY. GO, TAMMY, GO!" She can simply write out that she got an A on her paper: "GOOD JOB ON THE PAPER, TAMMY!"

Brain Gains #32a

"'Imagining' allows us to remember and mentally rehearse our intended movements. In fact, visualizing movement changes how our brain networks are organized, creating more connections among different regions. It stimulates brain regions involved in rehearsal of movement, such as the putamen located in the forebrain, priming the brain and body for action so that we move more effectively. Even picturing others in motion warms up the 'action brain' and helps us figure out what we want to do and how we can coordinate our actions with those around us. Over time, the brain learns our routine movements, allowing these actions to become more automatic and fine-tuned" (Lohr, 2015).

STRATEGY #4: INTRODUCE CHECKLISTS

Checklists stimulate your student to think part-to-whole or to think in the future that is connected to our cerebral cortex. They also reinforce the student's ability to sequence and helps him see the world abstractly when learning is from whole-to-part. Finally, checklists teach about beginnings, middles, and ends as well as setting goals and seeing the end result (e.g., "five things to do for finishing my report"). Once more, checklists feed into his ability to organize and manage time. Remember: An organized brain is an intelligent brain!

What Else Needs to Be Done? Completed Date/Time

1. Finished math homework: _____
2. Finished English homework: _____
3. Cleaned my room: _____

Included in the time element should be procrastination.

Brain Gains #33: The Reasons We Procrastinate

1. Not knowing what needs to be done
2. Not knowing how to do something
3. Not wanting to do something
4. Not caring if it gets done or not
5. Not caring when something gets done

6. Not feeling in the mood to do it
7. Being in the habit of waiting until the last minute
8. Believing that you work better under pressure
9. Thinking that you can finish it at the last minute
10. Lacking the initiative to get started
11. Forgetting
12. Blaming sickness or poor health
13. Waiting for the right moment
14. Needing time to think about the task
15. Delaying one task in favor of working on another

(Tuckman et al., 2008)

STRATEGY #5: ASSIGN HOUSEHOLD CHORES

All children should participate in the successful functioning of household chores because it teaches children to be a part of the organization of the household and/or how a successful home works. For example, children can help with the laundry, empty the dishwasher, or set the table, along with other tasks that involve preplanning, making lists, or arranging activities—all of which should be required of every child. Finally, post the chore list in the kitchen with assigned names and days that the chore is required.

John: Empty Dishwasher: Monday _____ Wednesday _____ Completed
John: Vacuum Bedroom: Tuesday _____ Thursday _____ Completed
Jane: Vacuum Bedroom: Monday _____ Wednesday _____ Completed
Jane: Empty Dishwasher: Tuesday _____ Thursday _____ Completed

STRATEGY #6: SCHOOL PREPARATION

On school nights, students need to have clothes, books, school supplies, and (possibly) lunch ready. Further, he should stay with a structured morning schedule: The student rises at the same time, brushes teeth, eats breakfast, leaves for school, and so on.

Once more, a structured routine is essential for school and life successes. For young children, parents can create a "pictorial chore chart" in their bedroom and bathroom. Add stars for each day when he can follow through with his routines. Add a reward if he achieves a certain number of stars for the week, such as a trip to a bookstore or a special gift at the local toy store.

STRATEGY #7: ORGANIZING FOR LIFE
The more organized and orderly you make your student's life, the more you support higher learning and intelligence and the frontal lobes. Examples include plastic containers for whatever they collect and closet organizers. Again, when you organize, you teach part-to-whole, which reinforces the prefrontal lobes seat of an organized brain.

STRATEGY #8: PLANNERS FOR THE FUTURE
Planners feed into your monthly calendar and/or whiteboards. In addition, planners will define school schedules and allow students to add important dates, homework assignments, and school activities.

STRATEGY #9: PORTFOLIOS
This is a no-brainer and something that needs to start early in your student's life. Create a portfolio with your student, and collect their most unique schoolwork, artwork, or whatever your student feels are important or relish. Once your student gets in the habit of saving schoolwork, artwork, and so on, he can carry this habit into middle and high school, when he can use his portfolio collections to support school projects. Lastly, he can use the portfolio if he plans on attending schools specializing in the arts, writing, and so on.

STRATEGY #10: HOMEWORK ROUTINES SHOULD NEVER BE ROUTINE
Your student's homework routine is essential to school success. First and foremost, he needs a special place to study. If in his bedroom, then that is the place he will go to study and complete homework. This should be *his area*, and you should try to keep this special learning place *his* learning area. Also, be sure he has a set time to begin and end homework (an idea would be to purchase a good clock). When he does not have homework, he can use this period as quiet time to read or go over and review the weeks' class notes. Finally, be sure to have his whiteboard and wall calendar nearby for reminders or simply to write notes to himself.

STRATEGY #11: HOMEWORK TOOLBOX
His homework toolbox should be filled with all the needed supplies for homework and school projects, such as glue, pencils, calculator, and scissors. DO

NOT LET OTHERS BORROW FROM HIS TOOLBOX! He will soon have his school supplies depleted, which will disrupt his homework schedule. Also, be sure to have a good dictionary, thesaurus, atlas, and any other reference and information books handy for quick and easy access.

STRATEGY #12: REWARDS FOR GOOD ORGANIZATIONAL SKILLS
Reward and provide support for organizational tasks done well. Your student may find organizing a challenge, so help him develop a routine, and give him a reward for a job well done. If an allowance is in play, it should be based on the child's age. I liked to give rewards to my children by taking them to a bookstore or out for an ice cream.

STRATEGY #13: ESTABLISHING TELEPHONE HOTLINES (MIDDLE/HIGH SCHOOL)
Get the names and phone numbers of three friends whom your student can call for homework or to participate in a study group. Be sure to select students based on good study skills and not simply close friends who will look at study groups as a time to socialize.

STRATEGY #14: SET UP A PARENT/TEACHER CONFERENCE
At the beginning of the school year, set up a time to meet with teachers about their homework policies as well as tests and grading. Also, ask how much time would be required for an average night's homework. (Note: For high school and middle school students, you can connect with teachers on back-to-school night and/or through emails.)

STRATEGY #15: CLASSROOM ROUTINES
Be sure to ask about your student's classroom routines regardless of whether he may try to discourage you or view it as prying. Also, schedule a meeting with his teacher at the end of the first progress report. What you do now will pay huge dividends in your student's future school and life success. Where is he sitting? When are tests scheduled? Let teachers know they can call you anytime to check in with you about changes in your student's behavior as well.

STRATEGY #16: WHAT TYPE OF LEARNING STYLE HAS YOUR STUDENT DISPLAYED?

As you will learn in chapter eight, "Learning Styles," some students are active learners, others are reflective learners, and still others may exhibit a preferred verbal or spatial intelligence. (Note: Parents can reference chapter three in my second book in the Brain Smart Trilogy titled *Brain Changing: Major Advancements in How Children Learn*).

Again, the wise parent will be aware of different learning styles and/or multiple intelligence. In addition, parents will learn the optimum times for how and when their students learn best. Do they exhibit higher-focusing abilities during specific time periods such as directly after school, after play, or after dinner? Further, where are his most-effective study areas? His bedroom, at the kitchen table, or in the living room? Also, does he prefer to study lying down or sitting? Finally, does he work best with music playing or in silence?

Brain Gains #34: Benefits of Studying with Music?

"More and more, students are bringing headphones with them to libraries and study halls. But does it actually help to listen to music when studying? While the so-called Mozart effect, a term coined from a study that suggested listening to music could actually enhance intelligence, has been widely refuted, there are still many benefits of listening to music while studying:

- Music that is soothing and relaxing can help students to beat stress or anxiety while studying.
- Background music may improve focus on a task by providing motivation and improving mood. During long study sessions, music can aid endurance.
- In some cases, students have found that music helps them with memorization, likely by creating a positive mood, which indirectly boosts memory formation.
- There are drawbacks to listening to music while studying. Despite the benefits mentioned, studies have shown that music is oftentimes more distracting than it is helpful.
- Students who listen to music with lyrics while completing reading or writing tasks tend to be less efficient and come away having absorbed less information.
- Loud or agitated music can have adverse effects on reading comprehension and on mood, making focus more difficult.

ORGANIZATION AND TIME MANAGEMENT

- Students who use music to help them memorize sometimes need to listen to music while taking the test to reap the benefits of this study method. In the silent test-taking environment, these students may find it more difficult to recall the information.

"Ultimately, the effects of music on study habits are dependent on the student and their style of learning. If easily distracted, students should most likely avoid music so they can keep their focus on their work. Conversely, students who function better as multitaskers may find that music helps them to concentrate better.

"Some students actually work best with background music because it is like white noise, and for some students, white noise actually grounds their energy and improves focusing ability" (Davis, n.d.).

STRATEGY #16: SUNDAY DINNERS
Sunday family dinners are a good way to go over the upcoming week's activities, such as soccer practices, major tests, and projects. It is also a good time for family appreciations.

STRATEGY #17: CONTRACTS
Some students will require a contract because not all students are able to stick to schedules, goal achievement, and so forth.

Brain Gains #35

Please Google *Dr. David Sortino: Contracts, Adolescence and Family Values.*

Brain Gains #36

Please Google *Rory Donaldson, Master Teacher: Contracts That Put You in Charge of Learning.*

Brain Gains #37

Please Google *Dr. David Sortino: Transitioning to Middle School.*

Brain Gains #38

It is imperative that your student learns the rules underlying school attendance. For example, tardiness can affect graduation requirements because excessive tardiness can lead to loss of credits, which can affect a senior's eligibility for graduation.

Brain Gains #39
Please see the Appendix for an example of a public school attendance policy.

STRATEGY #18: MIDDLE AND HIGH SCHOOL STUDY SCHEDULE AND PREPARATION CHECKLIST

Place a check in each box that affirms facets of your study schedule and preparation.

A. STUDY SKILLS AND PREPARATION

1. _____ I write down my assignments using an assignment sheet and/or notebook.
2. _____ I check my assignment sheets and/or notebook before I go home.
3. _____ I remember to write down all instructions for each assignment.
4. _____ I set study goals for myself before I begin to study.
5. _____ I have a specific study schedule that I can stick to.
6. _____ I regularly review my study schedule to make sure it is working.

TOTAL SCORE FOR PART A: _____

B. STUDY AREA

1. _____ I have a special place or time to study where/when I can be alone.
2. _____ I study sitting at a desk or table.
3. _____ I try to keep distractions (television, radio, cell phones, iPods, computer, etc.) to a minimum.
4. _____ I have learned to block out interruptions (shutting off phones as well as placing a "Do Not Disturb" sign on my door).
5. _____ I have methods that bring back my attention if I begin to daydream or become distracted.
6. _____ I have the materials I need to study at home, such as pens, paper, pencils, dictionary, and/or other resource materials and books.

TOTAL SCORE FOR PART B: _____

C. STUDY TIME

1. _____ I have determined what time of day is best for me to study.
2. _____ I study for 30 to 45 minutes before I take a 10- to 15-minute break. (Note: "Active" or "reflective" learners should take note.)
3. _____ I use odd times during the day for studying. I include weekend study time as part of my schedule.
4. _____ I am careful that my out-of-school activities do not cause me to fall behind in my schoolwork or study schedule.
5. _____ My schedule allows enough time for sleep, play, exercise, and socializing.
6. _____ I use classroom time wisely. (Note: Be aware of where you sit and by whom you sit because it is easy to become distracted by classmates and seating arrangements).

TOTAL SCORE FOR PART C: _____

D. STUDY DEADLINES

1. _____ I study for tests early rather than waiting until the last minute.
2. _____ I begin working on long-term assignments early rather than wait until the last minute (projects, term papers, book reports, etc.).
3. _____ I hand in my papers on time. (Note: Be sure to speak to your teachers about late work and whether they accept late work or not. Some teachers have different policies.)

TOTAL SCORE FOR PART D: _____

YOUR FINAL SCORE: _____

    8–12: You prepare ahead of time for tests and projects. (Top dog)

    4–7: You need to be more timely when completing study tasks. (Not bad)

    0–4: You wait until the last minute to complete tasks. (Big trouble)

TOTAL SCORE: _____

TOTAL YOUR SCORE FOR PARTS A THROUGH D: _____

YOUR TOTAL SCORE IS: _____

> 70–92: Congratulations! You manage your time well.
>
> 47–69: Your time is adequately used, but by setting some goals, your time can be more productive.
>
> 23–46: You need to look at your time-management strategies and set some goals for improvement.

Add up your score for each part. The following is a simple way for you to discover your strengths and weaknesses when it comes to how you manage your time.

Score Analysis:

A. STUDY SKILLS AND PREPARATION

YOUR SCORE: _____

> 19–24: You are prepared to study.
>
> 13–18: Your study area is okay, but it could be better.
>
> 7–12: You need to work on your study schedule and preparation for study.

B. STUDY AREA:

YOUR SCORE: _____

> 19–24: You have a good place to study.
>
> 13–18: Your study place is okay, but you can do better.
>
> 7–12: You really need to improve your place of study and work on limiting interruptions.

Brain Gains #40

Again, Ernest Hemingway wrote his novels standing up at his fireplace mantel, while Henry Wadsworth Longfellow wrote his epic poems standing at his desk.

4

Windows of Opportunity

Brain formation is dependent on brain activity, and because the developing brain is plastic, each and every early childhood experience stimulates, both positively and negatively, its neural connections. There are windows of opportunity when your child's brain is highly susceptible to environmental experiences.

—Huffington Post, *2014*

"Windows of opportunity" for the newborn infant and beyond begins at conception. Therefore, the richer the environment (i.e., the womb), the *denser* the interconnections among the brain cells. Further, from ages three to 12 is when the window of opportunity and brain stimulation is greatest (Diamond and Hopson, 1998).

Brain Gains #41

"The Head Start Project is the most important social and educational investment in children, families, and communities that the United States has ever undertaken. The project was launched in 1965 as a comprehensive child development program. Over the past 50 years, it has provided a window of opportunity for success in life to more than 32 million low-income and other vulnerable children and their families across the United States. Head Start has remained strong in the face of changing political and fiscal climates because it has continually improved the services it delivers to children and families and responded to the changing needs of local communities" (NHSA, n.d.).

Brain Gains #42

Please Google *Dr. David Sortino: Head Start: When a No Brainer Becomes a Brainer.*

MOTOR DEVELOPMENT

The early development of motor skills causes higher functioning of the brain at an early age when the child is most receptive to motor skill development or muscle memory (i.e., kinesthetic intelligence). Therefore, talk to other parents whose children have had teachers, trainers, or coaches who have been recognized for excellence in their fields. Finally, consult with schools and/or programs that cater to your child's kinesthetic intelligence, such as Montessori, Steiner, and so on.

Moreover, a suggestion to parents of children interested in playing a sport is to read John Wooden's book *Game Plan for Life* (2005). Wooden was a highly respected and successful UCLA basketball coach who won 10 NCAA basketball championships in 12 years! He believed that winning and losing, although important, should be secondary to skill and character development. Also, Wooden coached his players with the intention that they become teachers of the game, which resulted in many of his players becoming successful coaches at all levels of the game. For example, instead of first asking the child, "Did you win or lose the game?" we might ask the child, "Did you improve with your passing or dribbling skills?" or, "What did you learn from the game?" and, above all, "Did you have fun?"—which should be the baseline for a teacher or coach.

EMOTIONAL CONTROL

The emotional brain is especially dominant by ages two to three and often called "The First Renaissance" because the limbic system develops more rapidly than the frontal lobe (i.e., logic in decision-making). Hence, when and why the "terrible twos" occur. Interestingly, the same can be said of adolescence, or "The Second Renaissance." According to Sheryl Feinstein, author of *Inside the Teenage Brain: Parenting a Work in Progress* (2009), "Their decision-making can be overly influenced by emotions, because their brains rely more on the limbic system (the emotional seat of the brain) than the more rational prefrontal cortex."

Brain Gains #43

"The brain of a young teen isn't just a bigger version of a younger kid's brain. It isn't a smaller version of an adult's, either. As children grow, their brains morph. Some areas mature and build connections. Other areas may disconnect or get trimmed away. Brain areas that process emotions mature very quickly. The prefrontal cortex does not. This leaves the emotion-processing centers on their own for a while" (Brookshire, 2016).

VOCABULARY

Babies begin to babble as early as two months; by eight months, they can say "Mama." My daughter's first word was "moon," which was in response to my pointing to a moon-like ornament hanging in her room. At 18 to 20 months, a toddler can learn 10 new words per day or develop a vocabulary of 900 words by age three. At age five, his vocabulary increases from 2,500 to 3,000 words (Sousa, 2005).

Moreover, parents should read aloud to their children or use "Echo Reading" when reading to the child. For example, after you read a sentence, the child will repeat what you just read. Also, "Choral Reading," "Reading Theatre," and "The Read Aloud" programs are other good programs to support early reading skills.

Brain Gains #44

Please Google *Dr. David Sortino: Increasing Reading Fluency with Beginning Readers.*

SPOKEN LANGUAGE

Spoken language begins at birth and slowly tapers off between the ages of 10 to 12. Therefore, if you want to start a child in another language, start early! On the other hand, for language enrichment, "drama camps" are an excellent strategy for some children. In addition, "story listening tapes" in the car also work well. Furthermore, the next time you take your child for a stroll in a carriage, have the child face you so you can talk or sing to your child while you walk.

Studies show that parents are spending more time with their children than parents did 50 years ago:

"In 1965, mothers spent a daily average of 54 minutes on childcare activities, while moms in 2012 averaged almost twice that at 104 minutes per day.

Fathers' time with children nearly quadrupled—1965 dads spent a daily average of just 16 minutes with their kids, while today's fathers spend about 59 minutes a day caring for them.

"These numbers include parents from all education levels. When the researchers broke out the 2012 data into two categories—parents with a college education versus parents without—they found quite a difference. College-educated moms spent an estimated 123 minutes daily on childcare, compared with 94 minutes spent by less-educated mothers. Fathers with a college degree spent about 74 minutes a day with their kids, while less-educated dads averaged 50 minutes" (Harriman and Ashbach, 2016). Note: Read more at: https://phys.org/news/2016-09-today-parents-kids-moms-dads.html#jCp.

Brain Gains #44a

"One of the first windows of opportunity for language comes early in life. We know that infants start out able to distinguish the sound of all languages, but by six months of age, they are no longer able to recognize sounds that are not heard in their native tongue. As infants hear the patterns of sound in their own language, a different cluster of neurons in the auditory cortex of the brain responds to each sound. By six months of age, infants will have difficulty picking out sounds they have not heard repeated often" (Shiver, 2001).

Brain Gains #45

State Boards of Education should require all parents to attend child development lectures and/or classes provided by their school districts or local colleges and universities.

MATH AND LOGIC

According to brain scientists, children have an elementary understanding of numbers at birth (Butterworth, 1999). They understand the difference between two of something and three of something. Further, a fully functioning language ability is not needed to support numerical thinking (Brannon and Van der Walle, 2001). Additionally, find a math camp or a math tutor so that your child can have fun with math. It is called "enrichment" and connects with the brain's hippocampus, which is the "seat of bonding." Finally, a Montessori curriculum is an excellent alternative for students who express a high kinesthetic and/or mathematical intelligence.

Brain Gains #46

"As described by the National Council of Teachers of Mathematics, mathematical power includes the ability to explore, conjecture, and reason logically; to solve routine problems; to communicate about and through mathematics; and to construct ideas within mathematics and between other intellectual activity. Mathematical power also involves the development of personal self-confidence and a disposition to seek, evaluate, and use quantitative and spatial information in solving problems and in making decisions. Students' flexibility, perseverance, interest, curiosity, and intuitiveness also affect the realization of mathematical power.

"Mathematics is second only to reading in the amount of time spent and money budgeted in elementary school curricula" (Ruby, 2002).

INSTRUMENTAL MUSIC

At age three, most toddlers have the manual dexterity to play a piano. "Music instruction appears to accelerate brain development in young children, particularly in the areas of the brain responsible for processing sound, language development, speech perception, and reading skills, according to initial results of a five-year study by USC neuroscientists" (Gersema, 2016). Therefore, parents should provide music lessons and/or seek schools that promote music and/or integrate the arts as part of their curriculum (e.g., Steiner Schools).

Brain Gains #47

The Mozart Effect: fact or fiction? The jury is still out as to whether or not listening to Mozart increases a child's intelligence, particularly when played to infants. My opinion is that good music is like good food, so it makes sense to feed the temporal lobe areas of the child's brain.

A challenge that students face in today's schools is the lack of an academic arts curriculum due to mandated curriculums, testing, shortened school years, and/or budget cuts. Brain scientists have documented that when you combine the arts with the academics, you not only stimulate greater learning potential and intelligence, but you also support the psychological aspects of confidence and self-esteem, as well as create more of an emotional commitment to learning (Gazzaniga, 2008).

Brain Gains #48

Brain circuits involved in musical improvisation are shaped by systematic training, leading to less reliance on working memory and more extensive connectivity within the brain (Pinto, 2018).

A study by Edward Fiske demonstrated that students in arts-based youth organizations achieved higher scores when compared to the standard school population on questions dealing with self-worth, personal satisfaction, and overall student achievement. Also, well-designed and executed arts programs integrated into the academic curriculum have been correlated with higher academic performance, workplace success, and overall positive influence on the lives of students (Fiske, 1999).

Successful art-centered curriculum research has demonstrated that access to and participation in the arts helps decrease and prevent negative behavior of at-risk youth (NSBA, 2009).

Another study of high school student achievement scores demonstrated that students who were enrolled in art classes achieved higher math, verbal, and/or composite SAT scores than students who did not take art classes. The greatest improvement with SAT scoring occurred with students who had taken *four or more years* of art classes, scoring 102 points higher on their SATs than students who took one-half year or less. SAT scores increased consistently with the addition of more years of art classes. In other words, the more years of art classes, the higher the SAT scores (College Board, 2010).

Brain Gains #49

"By encouraging creativity and imagination, we are promoting children's ability to explore and comprehend their world and increasing their opportunities to make new connections and reach new understandings" (Early Arts, 2017).

Furthermore, a study identified students who took acting classes. This study had the strongest correlation with high verbal SAT scores. Acting classes and music history, theory, or appreciation had the strongest relationships with high math SAT scores, and all classifications of arts classes were found to have a significant relationship with both higher verbal and math SAT scores. Lastly, students with one year or more of art and music classes averaged 528 on the writing portion of the test—40 points higher than students with one-half year or less of arts/music classes, or 466 points (College Board, 2001).

Brain Gains #50

Please Google *Dr. David Sortino: How the Arts Can Raise Student Achievement.*

5
Listening Intelligence

Did you know that most of the work of hearing is done NOT by your ears but by your brain? It's true that sounds are taken in by our ears, and they must function properly for us to hear, but processing the sounds into meaning is solely a function of our brains. What is the difference between hearing and listening? We hear a lot, but we only process what we listen to, and that takes brainpower. Thus, training our brains to listen becomes essential if we are to engage with the world around us.

—*California Hearing Center, 2018*

If you notice a certain look in your child's eyes that says they are not listening, it might be that they simply lack the ability to "sequence your conversation," and it might be time for some assessment of their listening ability.

Brain Gains #50a

One well-known assessment used to define the strengths and weaknesses of a child's auditory listening skills is called the TAPS, which stands for Test for Auditory and Perceptual Skills (Martin and Brownell, 2005). The TAPS method assesses the child's auditory skills necessary for the development, use, and understanding of language commonly utilized in academic and everyday activities.

Understanding your child's listening or auditory skills raises the bar for parent and/or teacher communication. For example, we often expect children to listen to us, regardless of our purpose or subject matter discussed. However, there may be other factors that can affect their ability to listen besides interest. For example, there is the "decibel level" of a parent yelling in frustration or even the time factor. According to some experts, after the first few minutes of a lecture, the child's listening ability decreases rapidly. Also, research has shown that children tend to remember the beginning and the end of a lecture (primacy/recency effect) but not the middle.

Brain Gains #51

"When we talk about the 'primacy effect' and the 'recency effect,' we are talking about the theory and application of the following: 'The *Primacy Effect* . . . you remember some things at the beginning of a list because it occurred first. There is the beginning, a long middle that blurs together, and now it is the end. The *Primacy Effect* is the beginning. You remember it because that is where you started. The Recency Effect is the finish. You remember the end the best'" (Morrison, 2015).

In addition, there are other factors, such as making eye contact, speaking to the child rather than down, or taking the child's perspective, and so forth.

Brain Gains #52

Please Google *Raising Good Children by Dr. Thomas Lickona.*

Again, perhaps some children's brains are simply not set up to listen or to sequence conversations as we would expect. In other words, suppose listening strengths and weaknesses might be the result of the child's multiple intelligence or learning styles as proposed by some theorists. Before parents become frustrated with the child's listening inabilities, they need to take note as to why some children are better at listening and others are not.

Brain Gains #53

Speech and music are domains with different representations. Nonetheless, they both use sounds as their building blocks. An interesting question is whether experience or training with sounds in one domain can influence sound processing outside that particular domain. Numerous studies have thus far shown that music training sharpens not only music but also speech sound-processing abilities (Asaridou and McQueen, 2013).

On the other hand, there are those students who function with what is described as a "global learning style" or "spatial intelligence." These students are highly visual and see pictures rather than words, or wholes rather than parts, and often have difficulty sequencing or following a conversation or words in a series.

Therefore, before you become frustrated with the child's listening inabilities, you might want to think about listening strategies and assessments. It could save you and the child hours of frustration and enhance relationship building as well as increased learning and intelligence.

I. STRATEGIES TO IMPROVE EARLY CHILDHOOD LISTENING SKILLS

When we take a developmental perspective to intelligence and learning, we should also start our listening strategies with early childhood. The following suggestions support a developmental approach that can facilitate higher stages of learning and intelligence (UNICEF Belize, 2014).

Strategy #1: Squat to Your Child's Level

Before giving your child directions, squat to your child's eye level, and engage your child in eye-to-eye contact to get his attention. Teach him how to focus: "Mary, I need your eyes; Billy, I need your ears." Offer the same body language when listening to the child. Be sure not to make your eye contact so intense that your child perceives it as controlling rather than connecting.

Strategy #2: Address the Child

Open your request with the child's name: "Lauren, will you please . . . ?"

Strategy #3: Stay Brief

Use the "one-sentence rule": Put the main directive in the opening sentence. The longer you ramble, the more likely your child could become parent-deaf. Too much talking is a very common mistake when discussing an issue. It gives the child the feeling that you're not quite sure what it is you want to say. If he can keep you talking, he can get you sidetracked.

Strategy #4: Keep It Simple

Use short sentences with one-syllable words. Listen to how kids communicate with each other and take note. When your child shows that glazed, disinterested look, you are no longer being understood.

Brain Gains #54

Yet again, we often remember only the beginnings and endings of a direction and not the middle; therefore, keep it short and sweet.

Strategy #5: Ask Your Child to Repeat the Request Back to You

If he can't do that, it's too long or too complicated.

Strategy #6: Make an Offer the Child Can't Refuse

You can reason with a two- or three-year-old, especially to avoid power struggles: "Get dressed so you can go outside and play." Offer a reason for your request that is to the child's advantage and one that is difficult to refuse. This gives him a reason to move out of his power position and do what you want him to do.

Brain Gains #55

"Two-year-olds are struggling with their reliance on their parents and their desire for independence. They're eager to do things on their own, but they're beginning to discover that they're expected to follow certain rules. The difficulty of this normal development can lead to inappropriate behavior, frustration, out-of-control feelings, and tantrums" (Hoecker, 2019).

Brain Gains #56

As your child grows older and is able to entertain more than one perspective, most offers will be based on fairness, so be willing to compromise. (Note: Please see Dr. Thomas Lickona's *Raising Good Children* [1983].)

Strategy #7: Be Positive

Instead of "No running," try "Inside, we walk; outside, you may run."

Strategy #8: Begin Your Directives with "I Want . . . "

Instead of "Get down!" say, "I want you to get down." Instead of "Becky gets a turn," say, "I want you to let Becky have a turn now." This works well with children who want to please but don't like being ordered. By saying, "I want . . .", you give a reason for compliance rather than just an order.

Strategy #9: Say, "When . . . , then . . . "

"When you get your teeth brushed, then we'll begin the story." "When your work is finished, then you can watch TV." Using the word "when" implies that you expect obedience, and it works better than "if," which suggests that the child has a choice when you don't mean to give him one.

Brain Gains #57

Boys and girls hear differently. When you speak in a loud tone, girls interpret this as yelling; they think you are mad, and they may shut down. Also, girls have a more finely tuned aural structure. They can hear higher frequencies and are more sensitive to sound. Teachers need to watch the tone of their voices. Boys respond to sounds associated with matter-of-factness, even excitement. Since a boy's hearing is not as sensitive as a girl's, they should sit at the front of the class.

Strategy #10: "Legs First, Mouth Second!"

Instead of hollering, "Turn off the TV—it's time for dinner," walk into the room where your child is watching TV, join in with your child's interests for a few minutes, and then, during a commercial break, have your child turn off the TV. Going to your child conveys you're serious about your request; otherwise, children interpret this as a mere preference.

Strategy #11: Give Choices!

"Do you want to put your pajamas on or brush your teeth first? Red shirt or blue shirt?"

Strategy #12: Speak Developmentally Correct Directives

The younger the child, the shorter and simpler your directives should be. Consider your child's level of understanding. For example, a common error parents make is asking a three-year-old, "Why did you do that?" Even adults can't always answer that question about their behavior. Try instead, "Let's talk about what you did."

Strategy #13: Speak Politely

Even a two-year-old can learn "Please." Expect your child to be polite. Children shouldn't feel manners are optional. Speak to your children the way you want them to speak to you.

Strategy #14: Speak Psychologically Correct Sentences

Threats and judgmental openers are likely to put the child on the defensive. "You" messages make a child clam up. "I" messages are non-accusing. Instead of "You'd better do this," or "You must...," try, "I would like..." or "I am so pleased when you..." Instead of "You need to clear the table," say, "I need you to clear the table." Don't ask a leading question when a negative answer is not an option. Instead of "Will you please pick up your coat?" say, "Pick up your coat, please."

Strategy #15: Write It Out!

Reminders can devolve into nagging so easily, especially for preteens who feel being told what to do puts them in the defensive category. Without saying a word, you can communicate anything you need said. Talk with a pad and pencil: Leave humorous notes for your child, and then sit back and watch it happen.

Strategy #16: Talk the Child Down

The louder your child yells, the softer you respond. Let your child ventilate while you interject timely comments: "I understand," or "Can I help?" Sometimes just having a caring listener available will wind down the tantrum. If you come in at his level, you have two tantrums to deal with. Be the adult for him.

Strategy #17: Settle the Listener

Before giving your directive, restore emotional equilibrium; otherwise, you are wasting your time. Nothing sinks in when a child is an emotional wreck.

Strategy #18: Replay Your Message

Toddlers need to be told a thousand times, and children under two have difficulty internalizing your directives. Most three-year-olds begin to internalize directives so that what you ask begins to sink in. As your child gets older, do less and less repeating. Preteens regard repetition as nagging.

Strategy #19: Let Your Child Complete the Thought
Instead of "Don't leave your mess piled up," try "Matthew, think of where you want to store your soccer stuff." Letting the child fill in the blanks is more likely to create a lasting lesson.

Strategy #20: Use Rhyming Rules
"If you hit, you must sit." Get your child to repeat rules. "Move your feet, lose your seat!"

Strategy #21: Give Likable Alternatives
"You can't go by yourself to the park, but you can play in the neighbor's yard."

Strategy #22: Give Advanced Notice
"We are leaving soon. Say bye-bye to the toys, bye-bye to the girls . . . "

Strategy #23: How to Open Up a Closed Child
Carefully chosen phrases open up closed little minds and mouths. Stick to topics that you know, such as specifics. Instead of "Did you have a good day at school today?" try "What is the most fun thing you did today?"

Strategy #24: Use "When you . . . , I feel . . . because . . ."
"When you run away from Mommy in the store, I feel worried because you might get lost."

Strategy #25: Close the Discussion
If a matter is really closed to discussion, say so: "I'm not changing my mind about this. Sorry." You'll save wear and tear on both you and your child (Doctor Sears, 2018).

II. STRATEGIES FOR HOME AND SCHOOL: LATE CHILDHOOD AND OLDER

Each day, a student is given instructions, information, and directions by many individuals, particularly teachers and parents. Good listening skills are a prerequisite for life and school success, so it is never too early to learn the valuable skill of listening as the basis of tapping in to learning potential and true intelligence. As students become better listeners, they will be able to learn, understand, and remember more, and generally, they do better in school. What follows are strategies and assessments for developing good listening skills.

We need to be aware that no student or child wants to be overmanaged. The following points should be considered as a potpourri of information for successful listening skills.

Strategy #1: When They Are Fearful to Ask the Teacher to Repeat Directions

All students need to develop good listening skills. This includes an understanding of what they are being asked or what they are expected to know. A common student listening problem is a fear of asking questions or participating in classroom discussions. For some students, asking relevant questions is one of the most difficult skills to develop because many students often feel intimidated by the teacher or have a fear of speaking in large groups.

Therefore, the student and parent need to meet with the teacher to develop some basic strategies that can help the student use his/her listening skills more effectively. For example, teachers can set up cues, such as student and teacher making eye contact to let the teacher know when the student needs to have the teacher repeat directions or assignments. As you will learn in chapter eight, certain learning styles support good/bad listening skills and others do not. For example, the "global learner" or the "spatial learner" hears information abstractly or sees the big picture first. Such students often have problems sequencing communication or following directions.

Strategy #2: Listening to Follow a Sequence

Again, we often remember the beginning and end of a conversation and forget the middle. At home, parents can have their student practice repeating what they just said. However, be sure to keep it simple, so that it doesn't appear negative or sarcastic, such as, "What did I just tell you?" or "Why don't you ever listen?" For younger children, parents can also play the "step game" by asking the child to explain the different steps, such as making the bed or setting the table. When you are driving in a car, have your child sequence the directions to arriving at your intended location. You are training their brain to recognize that sequencing (i.e., visually/orally) is a critical skill for successful listening skills, as well as for effective learning and intelligence.

Strategy #3: Listening for the Main Idea

Have your child practice listening for the main ideas of a lesson when the teacher is speaking or have them look for visual cues. Teachers often write out topics so students can visually clue in to what lesson is being taught. When your student can focus on what is being said or discussed, he will stand a better chance of answering questions on the topic. Also, he will be ready to ask questions for a greater understanding of the topic being discussed. For younger children, parents can practice this exercise at home by presenting an idea, and then letting the child guess what the topic might be.

For example, one subject might be cooking a meal. However, the parent does not tell the child what meal is being cooked. Instead, the parent can tell the child all the ingredients, and the child can try to guess the meal. Another strategy is for the parent to plan a car trip, and then to tell the child all the places they will need to pass through to get to their destination. Finally, the child has to guess the destination.

Strategy #4: Listen for Supporting Details

The student can listen for supporting details after he has identified the main idea. Also, the student should identify and try to remember the important details first and mentally ignore the unimportant details. Parents can teach the child to color-code their assignments or lessons by personalizing the main idea. (Note: This is good for visual learners.) If the exercise is discussing a particular individual, parents should try to show a photo of the individual, or at least be descriptive. For example, Benjamin Franklin had long white hair that grew down to his shoulders and, by the way, he invented bifocals.

Strategy #5: Simply Listening to a Lesson or Directions Is Not Enough

Students need to consider other factors that can affect their ability to listen and understand. The following listening strategies teach students about lecture content.

Strategy #6: Know When the Speaker Is Giving you a Fact

Know when the speaker is giving you a fact (i.e., an absolute truth) or an opinion (i.e., a personal point of view). "Facts" are statements that usually can be proven; "opinions" are personal views or ideas about a particular topic. To tell whether a statement is a fact or an opinion, ask yourself this question: Can this statement be proven? If it can, then it probably is a fact.

Conversely, an opinion is a belief or attitude about something that isn't necessarily based on facts. Lastly, a person may agree with an opinion, but that does not mean that the opinion is based on fact or is true.

Strategy #7: Emotional Appeals

Know when the speaker is making an emotional appeal to you. Perhaps the speaker has strong feelings about a topic. However, this does not mean the speaker is right, though he may want you to think or feel he does. For example, "Congress wants to pass a healthcare bill that is simply too expensive. Instead, we need to stick to the same programs that we have always maintained. For instance, I will not be able to see my own doctor if this bill goes through. Also, I will never get the care I need . . . I do not care if the AMA supports it. What do doctors know anyway?!"

Strategy #8: Drawing Conclusions

After your student has listened to someone present arguments about a topic, your student should be able to come to his own conclusions about the topic that may or may not agree with the speaker. For example, "Vietnam was the right war to fight, even though over 50,000 American lives were lost. We did it to save the Vietnamese people . . ."

Strategy #9: Listen with a Purpose

Know what you want to learn from the speaker. For example, "Marijuana should be legalized because many more people die from drinking alcohol! Over 20,000 people die in drunk-driving accidents. If alcohol is legal, then why not marijuana?"

Strategy #10: Maintain Eye Contact

Teach your student that if he/she is looking at the speaker, their attention will be on what is being said, and it will be easier to block out distractions.

Strategy #11: Visualize What Is Being Said
Create a picture in your mind of what the speaker is describing.

Strategy #12: Take Notes
Keep the notes brief. Have your students write down the main ideas or key words. Your student can use his notes for reviewing afterward or for questioning the speaker about anything that is unclear to him.

Strategy #13: Predict Questions
Have your student identify the most important points. For example, have him imagine the questions that the teacher might ask regarding the topic. Daily practice is needed to become a better listener.

Strategy #14: Try the TQLR Method
Tune in (T), question (Q), listen (L), and then review (R). Emphasize the importance to your student of not dividing his attention between the speaker and the neighboring student. If he wishes to absorb the material, he needs to focus on the speaker.

Strategy #15: Be an Active Listener
Don't let your mind wander to what you will be doing after school, next period, or how long until lunch. When you find your mind wandering, think about the main idea of the lecture, or try to remember one important point that you will take away from the lecture.

Strategy #16: Self-Listening Assessment (Middle and High School Students)
Note to reader: Periodically, have your student take this self-listening assessment to evaluate their strengths and weaknesses. Answer each question as honestly as you can.

SCORING: Determining How Good Your Listening Skills Are

- 3 points for each "always"
- 2 points for each "frequently"
- 1 point for each "occasionally"
- 0 point for each "never"

1. I am always aware of the purpose for listening: _____
2. Taking notes distracts me from listening: _____
3. I gather facts while listening: _____
4. I listen for the main idea: _____
5. I categorize the information: _____
6. I draw conclusions from what the speaker has said: _____
7. I can summarize what the speaker has said: _____
8. After listening, I am able to respond to questions asked: _____
9. I try to apply what I have learned: _____
10. Visual aids help me when listening: _____
11. I usually give all my attention to the speaker: _____
12. I doodle while listening: _____
13. I often dismiss material as too boring or uninteresting: _____
14. I often daydream: _____
15. I visualize (the material being given) while listening: _____
16. I get hung up on only one part of a lecture: _____
17. I maintain eye contact with the speaker: _____
18. I stay on track regardless of my interest: _____
19. The appearance and/or mannerisms of the speaker affect me: _____
20. Outside noises distract me from listening: _____

Rate your score below:

50 – 60 = Excellent Listening Skills

40 – 50 = Good Listening Skills

30 – 40 = Fair Listening Skills

20 – 30 = Poor Listening Skills

Total: _____

6

Memory

The more you know about your memory, the better you'll understand how you can improve it. Your baby's first cry, the taste of your grandmother's molasses cookies, the scent of an ocean breeze—these are memories that make up the ongoing experience of your life, they provide you with a sense of self. They're what make you feel comfortable with familiar people and surroundings, tie your past with your present, and provide a framework for the future. In a profound way, it is our collective set of memories—our "memory" as a whole—that makes us who we are.

—How Stuff Works!, *2018*

I. STAGES AND TYPES OF MEMORY

1. Sensory/Immediate

This is as immediate as it gets (usually in milliseconds) when it comes to retention. Can you recall what someone just said to you when you were not paying attention?

2. Working Memory

When temporary information is processed consciously, such as with classroom learning, we call it working memory.

Brain Gains #58

The human brain is hugely interconnected but with three major components: the cerebrum, the cerebellum, and the brain stem. Therefore, to help students with weak sensory/immediate and working memory skills, we should do the following:

- Break tasks into smaller chunks. One task at a time is best, if possible.
- Reduce the amount of material the student is expected to complete.
- Keep new information or instructions brief and to the point, and repeat in concise fashion for the student, as needed.
- Provide written directions for reference.
- Simplify the amount of mental processing required by providing several oral "clues" for a problem and writing keywords for each clue on the board or interactive whiteboard. This way, the student does not have to hold all of the information in his mind at once.
- Increase the meaningfulness of the material by providing examples students can relate to.
- Provide information in multiple ways: Speak it, show it, and create opportunities to physically work with it or model it.
- Develop routines, such as specific procedures for turning in completed assignments.
- Once a routine is practiced repeatedly, it becomes automatic and reduces the working memory (Alberta Education, 2013).

3. Long-Term Memory

Long-term memory is broken into two types: declarative and procedural. Declarative memory (i.e., conscious and explicit) is how we remember names, facts, and objects. Declarative is divided into two main areas of memory: episodic and semantic.

Episodic memory represents the past, such as your first hit in little league or your first kiss. Episodic memory is located in the hippocampus. The hippocampus is located in the brain's temporal lobe and is where episodic memories are formed and indexed for later access.

Brain Gains #59

One strategy to reinforce episodic memory is to help students construct a timeline. I have successfully used timelines with at-risk youth as a strategy to examine positive events in their life. Too often, at-risk students only dwell on failure or negative events when there is always something positive to flush out. Also, it feeds into long-term memory for students who have focusing problems.

Semantic memory is knowledge of facts and/or information. If you were in New York City, you would know that the Empire State Building was in New York. Semantic memory is located in the anterior temporal lobe, a region just in front of the ears and responsible for the understanding of words, meanings, and concepts. Strategies to improve semantic memory include remembering a series of words, such as memorizing the 50 states and their capitals.

Non-declarative memory (also called "implicit" or "behavioral" memory) is our memory for skills and habits, as well as emotional responses and reflexes. Further, declarative memory involves knowing "what," while non-declarative memory involves knowing "how." Everything you do, sense, think, or feel is set up, organized, and directed by the brain.

"Procedural (motor/cognitive) memory doesn't encode in the hippocampus. The encoding process takes place in other parts of the brain like the putamen, caudate nucleus, cerebellum, and the motor cortex. Skills that are acquired or learned are stored in the putamen. Instincts are stored in the caudate nucleus, and the cerebellum takes care of the timing and coordination" (Stuart-Squire and Zola-Morgan, 1988).

Strategies to stimulate procedural memory are formed through repetition and practice and associated with automatic sensorimotor behaviors that are so deeply embedded (muscle memory) that we are no longer aware of them. Once learned, these "body memories" allow us to carry out ordinary motor actions more or less automatically. Procedural is sometimes referred to as implicit memory because previous experiences aid in the performance of tasks without explicit and conscious awareness of these previous experiences, although it is more properly a subset of implicit memory (Zimmermann, 2014).

Perceptual representation system (i.e., sense data) is processed in many areas of the brain. Sound is processed in the temporal lobe on the side of the brain, vision is processed in the occipital lobe in the rear of the brain, taste and touch are processed in the parietal lobe on the side of the brain above the temporal lobe, and smell is processed in the midbrain near the memory centers.

"Your brain 'makes sense' out of all these different sensations when the data finally reaches the frontal lobes (in the front of the brain) and logical connections between incoming sense data are formed, such as recognition, memory recall, and pattern matching and prediction.

"Although sense data is processed all over the brain, it is the frontal lobes that use that data to make 'meaning' out of all the information your brain is receiving. The frontal lobes match incoming data from the senses against memory and expectations to give you a real-time picture of what is going on around you. If you want to improve your perceptual representation system, learn to play chess" (Kent, 2017).

Classical conditioning, also called "Pavlovian" (after the Russian behavioral psychologist Ivan Pavlov), represents the role classical conditioning connects with our learning brain. For example, when you hear a school bell, you know it is time to change classes. In the classroom, teachers need to be cognizant of the effects of classical conditioning on test anxiety and create a learning and test environment that reinforces a feeling of calm and focus. When a student takes a test in a low-pressure, positive environment over time, the classically conditioned response will become extinguished or disappear.

"Additionally, to use classical conditioning to the best effects of the technique, teachers have to integrate the process into the classroom learning model, which can take time away from the overall learning experience. The technique may only work with positive effects for some students; the other students may view it as a negative aspect of the classroom" (Renata, 2016).

Non-associative learning represents not paying attention, such as the ticking of a clock or not paying attention to music in the background while studying. Three types of non-associative learning are "habituation behavior," or when it is decreased due to repeated exposure to an innocuous stimulus. The second type is "sensitization," which is an increase in behavior due to exposure to a noxious stimulus such as a repeated annoyance stimulus as with a speaker's "OK"s. Perceptual learning is to process stimuli more rapidly and to distinguish similar from each other. A good example of how to measure non-associative learning might be how a lie detector works.

Brain Gains #60

I discovered how non-associative learning might help LH, ADHD, ADD, and RAD students to concentrate or focus. That is, during a silent learning exercise (e.g., math, writing, etc.), I tuned in to an all-day radio news program to calm my students' inability to focus. The key was always to make the broadcast almost inaudible, so that the students could not listen to what was being broadcasted. Scientists called this "white noise." Nevertheless, this tactic always worked for my most energetic, least focused students and actually helped them to focus. This could be why some kids actually study better when they have music playing.

II. ADDITIONAL TYPES OF MEMORY

Emotional memory is when you have a memory of a certain experience but cannot remember many facts about it. For example, we remember only the emotions associated with memories, such as sadness, fear, anger, happiness, and so on. Emotional memory is highly connected to your child's learning potential. For example, which early memory does your child have about his/her first school experiences? A fear some students have about reading in front of the class often elicits the words: "I feel dumb when I am asked to read out loud in class."

Emotional memory is associated with the limbic system, particularly the thalamus, amygdala, and hippocampus.

Flashbulb memories are long-lasting memories, such as what you were you doing on September 11, 2001.

Brain Gains #61

An exploding flashbulb captures many details. So-called flashbulb memories of intense emotional moments similarly freeze events (*National Geographic Guide*, 2016).

Short-term memory creates challenges for teachers and parents about how to increase your student's short-term memory and/or focusing time. For example, during a school lesson, children can hide for periods of time, tuning out the lesson or doing whatever their creative minds can do to escape boredom and appear to stay focused on the lesson at hand.

In addition, short-term memory is often used interchangeably with working memory, but the two should be utilized separately. Working memory refers to processes that are used to temporarily store, organize, and manipulate information. On the other hand, short-term memory refers only to the temporary storage of information in memory (Sousa, 2005). Once more, it is like receiving a phone number from the operator. Suppose you need to call your doctor for an appointment. You call information for a phone number but do not write it down. You make the call, but a few minutes later, you will forget the number.

Brain Gains #62

The first 20 minutes of the school day is considered the highest learning and/or focusing time for your student's learning brain. Therefore, mundane tasks such as taking milk counts, attendance, and so on should be put off until after the first 20 minutes of the school day.

We must remember that information can only be stored for 15 to 30 seconds, particularly if you do not use the information immediately (Atkinson and Shiffrin, 1971). In fact, the reason so many children are computer literate at such an early age is that the computer reinforces short-term memory or the brain's ability to respond to the 15- to 30-second focusing time.

Moreover, the purpose of helping children to focus longer is so they can move information from short-term memory to long-term memory. This is why hands-on, or kinesthetic activities, can reinforce longer focusing times because they stimulate the cerebellum (i.e., motor) as well as the hippocampus (i.e., emotional bonding).

Furthermore, kinesthetic activities allow students to form a more intense relationship (i.e., memory consolidation) with the learning experience, which can also stimulate greater learning potential. Again, to increase students' focusing time with early language learners, Montessori used sandpaper letters to teach the alphabet and/or phonemes by having the children trace their fingers over the letters as they said or sang them orally, supporting our multiple intelligence example.

Also, addressing other learning modalities or multiple intelligence, such as the visual or auditory, increases focusing and long-term memory consolidation due to connections with significant areas of the brain, particularly the limbic system and frontal lobes.

Brain Gains #63

"Intelligence is the wife, imagination is the mistress, memory is the servant"—(Victor Hugo).

Furthermore, the amount of information that can be stored in short-term memory can vary. For example, research suggests that individuals are capable of storing approximately four chunks (Cowan, 2001). That is, when you take individual pieces of information (i.e., chunks) and group them into larger units, you are supporting short-term memory as well as the amount of information you can remember.

Your social security number is three chunks, or, for example, 040-39-4009, and the same is true with most telephone numbers (415-821-8005) or birthdates (06-29-1950). Notice that most of these are in three chunks. Can you think of an example of four chunks?

Brain Gains #64

One reason speed-reading increases reading fluency and comprehension is due to chunking. With speed-reading, the reader is trained to focus on groups of words and not individual words, which increases fluency and reading comprehension. (Note: Please see chapter seven "Reading" for a basic description of our brain and the reading process.)

Brain Gains #65

Humans can retain five to nine pieces of information in their short-term memory. The amount of information increases when placed in chunks, which allows short-term memory to store about four chunks. Short-term memory processes and stores information for about 20 to 30 seconds. After this, information is either committed to long-term memory or lost altogether. Again, chunking is a good strategy to increase the capacity of short-term memory (Miller, 1956).

Working memory is temporary because we can assimilate only a few ideas at a time. Also, working memory operates out of the frontal lobe, the seat of organization and social interaction. For example, preschoolers can deal with one to three items of information at once and with an average of two items at best. Therefore, I would suggest parents begin reading to their preschoolers the Big Books reading series because it is highly visual and presents no more than three concepts at a time.

Brain Gains #66

The problem with working memory is that it can only deal with a few topics for a limited period of time. For pre-adolescents, working memory is five to 10 minutes; for adolescents to adults, it is 10 to 20 minutes (Russell, 1979).

III. MEMORY EXERCISES

Memory Exercise #1

Write this number down on a piece of paper: 3675829. Study the numbers for seven seconds. Now look away. Try to write down the numbers again. See what you remember and whether or not you used any special strategies to remember the numbers.

Studies show that the reason you might have had difficulty remembering all the numbers is because you might have treated each number or digit as a single item. Once more, this is why you need to learn strategies such as chunking (491-508-263-7). This is particularly important for elementary school teachers who must teach a concept that has more than one idea, such as the parts of speech, long division, and so on.

The same applies to high school students who must learn the biological terms of the human body, which would explain why the multiple intelligences (i.e., linguistic, visual, kinesthetic, etc.) or an interdisciplinary approach to teaching can increase learning.

Brain Gains #67

"'Chunking' or 'clustering' is the function of grouping information together related by perceptual features. This is a form of "semantic relation," such as types of fruit, parts of speech, or 1980s fashion. Chunking allows the brain to increase the channel capacity of the short-term memory; however, each chunk must be meaningful to the individual. There are many other memory consolidation techniques.

"The peg memory system creates a mental peg from an association, such as a rhyme, letter, or shape. Another memory technique is the "link system," where images are creating links, stories, or associations between elements in a list to be memorized" (Kahn Academy, 2018).

Memory Exercise #2

The brain is a pattern-seeking device: You only need to remember the first and last letters of each word to know its meaning!

Accroding to a resaerch stuyd at Cabmbrdiige Univresiyt, it deosn't mettar what odrer the lestter are palced. The only ipmortant thnig is that the frist and lsat letetr be in the rgiht pleace. The rest can be a toatl mses, and you can sltil raed it wthout a porbelm. Thsi is becuase the hueman mind deon not raed ervery word but the brani is a pattnrn sekeing devcie —David Sousa (*How the Brain Learns*, 2006)

Brain Gains #68

Yet again, the above memory exercise might explain why speed-reading exercises can help slow readers and increase reading fluency as well as comprehension. That is, the faster we read, the greater the brain's ability to move information from short-term to long-term memory.

Memory Exercise #3

In the exercise that follows, the letters must be spelled correctly and in their proper position. According to brain scientists, we will remember the first three to five words and the last one to two words (lines nine and 10) but have difficulty with the middle words (lines six through eight). This further reinforces the notion of classroom learning or why students remember the beginning and end of class lectures.

Most recently, studies have helped explain why this is so. The first items for new information are with the working memory's functional capacity, so they command our attention and are likely to be retained in semantic memory. As the learning episode concludes, items in working memory are sorted or checked to all or additional processing of the arriving final items, which are likely in working memory and will decay unless further rehearsed (Gazzaniga, 2008).

Cover the 10 groups of letters. Set a timer for 12 seconds. Look at the groups of letters for 12 seconds, then write down the letters as you studied them.

FEK   1. _____

KAL   2. _____

LIM   3. _____

RIN   4. _____

KEV   5. _____

NUL   6. _____

EMN   7. _____

BEI   8. _____

RAS   9. _____

FIO   10. _____

Another important point in support of working memory is the "phonological loop," or how the brain uses auditory mechanisms to stimulate working memory. For example, with hard-to-understand homework or writing assignments, it helps if your child reads aloud or sings important information as a strategy to convert working memory to long-term memory.

Brain Gains #69

Teachers should divide lessons into 15- to 20-minute chunks for maximum effect. The same strategy should apply for homework.

Long-Term Storage

"Most teachers believe that staying on task throughout the learning period is best. During 1994–1997, while an adjunct professor at Seton Hall University, I asked secondary teachers to conduct action research projects in their block schedule classrooms to determine if going off task between lesson segments (for example telling a joke or story, playing music, taking a rest break, or getting students up and moving around) resulted in more, less, or the same amount of attending (measured by the speed with which the students returned to task) than if they had stayed continuously on task" (Sousa, 2006). Please see the results below.

Once more, studies compared the degree of attending, defining on or off activities between 80-minute lesson segments of attending behavior for a block schedule. The study found that attending behavior diminished throughout the 80-minute block period. At 20 minutes the total number of minutes of student attentive behavior was 18 minutes, or 90 percent. After 40 minutes the total number of students' attending behavior dropped to 30 minutes, or 75 percent. At 80 minutes the total number of on-task minutes was 50 minutes, or 62 percent. The moral of the story? Teachers need to allow for short student breaks to keep students focused during the lesson segment if they go off-task between segments (Sousa, 2006).

Sense and Meaning

For anything to be remembered, the brain needs two basic components: Does it make sense, and does it have meaning? Brain scans have shown that when new learning is readily comprehensible to our senses and can be connected to meaning, there is substantially more cerebral activity followed by dramatically improved retention (Maguire et al., 1999).

Brain Gains #70

Sense data is processed in many areas of the brain: Sound is processed in the temporal lobe on the side of the brain; vision is processed in the occipital lobe in the rear of the brain; taste and touch are processed in the parietal lobe on the side of the brain above the temporal lobe; and smell is processed in the midbrain near the memory centers. Your brain "makes sense" out of all these different sensations when the data finally reaches the frontal lobes (in the front of the brain) and logical connections between incoming sense data are formed, such as recognition, memory recall, and pattern-matching and prediction.

Although sense data is processed all over the brain, it is the frontal lobes that use that data to make "meaning" out of all the information your brain is receiving. The frontal lobes match incoming data from the senses against memory and expectations to give you a real-time picture of what is going on around you (Kent, 2017).

In addition, sense and meaning are also most powerful when there is an emotional component to learning or when the learning is keyed in to the limbic system or hippocampus (i.e., bonding) and sent to long-term storage brain centers (i.e., multiple intelligences).

Brain Gains #71

Please see chapter 10, "Keys to Right-Brain Teaching Techniques to Support a Driver's Education Lesson."

REM, Sleep, and Memory

What the student has learned during the day is most dramatic during deep sleep, when memory attempts to consolidate information to long-term storage or memory. The bottom line: You will have converted working memory to long-term storage if you can remember the information after about 24 hours.

Brain Gains #72

"Researchers found that taking a nap about 45 to 60 minutes immediately after learning something new could boost your memory 500 percent! Further, exercise triggers high levels of a protein called "cathepsin B," which travels to the brain to trigger neuron growth and new connections in the hippocampus, an area in the brain believed to be critical for memory" (Pinola, 2019).

Brain Gains #73

Please Google *Dr. David Sortino: When Sleep Affects Learning Potential.*

According to a study by the Center for Disease Control and Prevention (2015), almost 70 percent of teens are not getting the recommended hours of sleep. This lack of sleep is associated with a variety of risky behaviors such as physical inactivity, alcohol consumption, cigarette smoking, fighting, sexual promiscuity, and excessive electronic and/or computer activity.

High school students participating in the 2007 National Youth Risk Behavior Survey were asked how much sleep they got on an average school night. Those who responded to getting less than eight hours were categorized as getting insufficient sleep. Those who got eight or more hours of sleep were categorized as getting sufficient sleep.

Researchers found that 68.9 percent of responders reported insufficient sleep on an average school night. Responders who reported insufficient sleep were also more likely to engage in risky behavior. Insufficient sleep was associated with the following 10 risky behaviors:

1. Drinking soft drinks one or more times a day. This does not include diet soft drinks.

2. Not participating in 60 minutes of physical activity five or more days a week
3. Using computers three or more hours each day
4. Physical fighting one or more times
5. Smoking cigarettes
6. Smoking marijuana
7. Drinking alcohol
8. Sexual activity
9. Feeling sad or hopeless
10. Seriously considering suicide

(Note: The above section is from SleepFoundation.org.)

Cognitive Belief System

An important point about long-term storage and/or long-term memory is the child's and/or student's cognitive belief system. For example, global warming can present many different arguments to students. That is, the child might base his global warming belief system on what he has learned in school versus what he has learned from his parents.

However, a common problem parents face during adolescence occurs when the child's home belief system is challenged by the outside world belief systems. Parents need to be able to adjust to such changes and be willing to compromise and be flexible with their thinking; otherwise, the quiet, respectful child that you knew of yesteryear will suddenly become argumentative and disrespectful to your values. (Note: Please see *Raising Good Children* by Thomas Lickona, [1983].)

Brain Gains #74

A major challenge to long-term memory is whether or not your student accepts or rejects new meanings or ideas. Are they willing only to experience learning that guarantees success? Children who have struggled with certain subjects (e.g., reading, mathematics, etc.) during the skill-building years (i.e., primary grades) often develop a lack of confidence and even a phobia when they are required to transfer information or knowledge to higher-order thinking or skill.

This is why it is critical that you define your child's learning preference and/or multiple intelligence to reinforce his learning strengths as well as learning weaknesses.

Retention

Another dilemma affecting your child's learning brain and school success is retention. Research shows that students will generally forget 50 percent to 80 percent of learned information (i.e., working memory) within 24 hours; after 30 days, it is 95 percent to 97 percent (RPCC, 2006). This is particularly true with classroom learning.

Once your child leaves the classroom, the major challenge to retention will be a lack of review. Specifically, the amount of time your student devotes to rehearsal (i.e., initial and secondary) and/or the type of rehearsals, rote or elaborative, that will affect long-term memory. Studies show that cramming for tests doesn't work. Students should review, review, and review some more.

Brain Gains #75

Please Google *Dr. David Sortino: When Choosing Wrong Answers Can Be Right.*

Initial Rehearsal

Initial rehearsal occurs as the information is processed through working memory. Again, working memory will be hindered if the learner does not make a connection with the sense and meaning of the information. In short, this is why teachers and parents need to employ additional modalities (i.e., multiple intelligences) as well as integrate the arts or hands-on learning to foster greater retention.

For instance, to teach children the multiplication tables (i.e., rote memorization), children can tap their feet as they rhythmically repeat the tables in time. The tapping and the rhythmic singing stimulate the child's kinesthetic intelligence and auditory center as well as the brain's cerebellum and limbic system.

With homework challenges, parents and students must review the antecedent learning steps to be sure the child knows how to connect old skills with new skills. Again, with long division, the child's antecedent steps would review short division, multiplication, and subtraction.

The Time Factor

Another important component of retention is the time factor, or whether your student immediately rehearses or reviews the information. Ultimately, your child's ability to connect working memory (i.e., classroom learning) to long-term memory is critical to school and life's successes.

Brain Gains #76

Mozart was able to play a 12-minute choral composition from memory after hearing it only twice!

Memory, Organization, Predictability, and School Schedules

These are key factors for attaching working memory (i.e., information) to long-term memory. A child who has been taught to apply his learning to an organized schedule can eliminate the inconsistency of disorganization to support better working memory, which could support long-term memory.

For example, one (obvious) recommendation is to hang your child's daily schedule on their bedroom wall so your student can visually connect with it on a daily basis.

Also, a large calendar is beneficial for recording important dates such as tests, due dates for homework assignments, and so on. Again, these are obvious suggestions but are often neglected. Finally, parents and/or caregivers should test their student on the weekly schedule to ensure they are attuned to all activities and events.

Brain Gains #77

Memories are more likely to be remembered if you combine information and emotion. Remember that the hippocampus is the only area of the brain where the regeneration of neurons occurs.

Rote Rehearsal

This occurs when the learner must produce the exact repetition of learned information into working memory. When children must memorize the multiplication tables and math formulas, they should also employ other learning modalities, such as kinesthetic and auditory intelligences, in order to increase the likelihood of long-term memory.

Another time, when the learner has to learn his times tables, he should apply kinesthetic learning methods, such as tapping his feet or clapping his hands while he sings his math facts. This will stimulate the cerebellum as well as the temporal lobe region, which increases the probability of greater long-term storage.

Elaborative Rehearsal

Elaborative rehearsal occurs when the student attaches new learning to old learning. We use rote rehearsal to memorize (e.g., times tables, states and capitals, etc.) but elaborative rehearsal to interpret and retain through personal interaction (Sousa, 2006). This is why cramming for tests or exams is the *weakest approach* for retention because we fail to attach new ideas, concepts, or solutions to old learning.

Rote Memorization

Students who attempt to use rote memorization without truly understanding the learned information can affect their ability to recall information. In other words, rote memorization might be acceptable for true/false or fill-in tests but weak when you have to think abstractly or expand on the information. Perhaps one reason only 35 percent of high school students scored at formal operational thinking, the cognitive stage of middle and high school curriculums (Reimer et al., 1999), is because their prior learning experiences centered only on rote memorization of factual information rather than elaborative rehearsal.

Therefore, if you want to remember facts such as the different types of political systems, use rote rehearsal. However, if you want greater memory storage, you need to use elaborative rehearsal such as personalizing the political systems or teaching the political systems to another student, as indicated below by the "Pyramid of Learning," which we will discuss here. The numbers describe the average percentage of material retained after 24 hours for each of the instructional methods.

Brain Gains #78

The Pyramid of Learning

Verbal processing = Lecture = 5%

Verbal Processing = Reading = 10%

Verbal and Visual Processing = Demonstration = 30%

Verbal and Visual Processing = Discussion Group = 50%

Doing = Practice by Doing = 75%

Doing = Teach/Others/Immediate Use of Learning = 90%

The average retention rate after 24 hours shows that students will only remember 5 percent of a lecture. Interestingly, the lecture format or verbal processing is a major approach in most high school classes. The second level, also associated with verbal processing, is "reading" with a 10 percent retention rate. The third level combines "verbal and visual processing or the audio-visual" and has a 30 percent retention rate.

The fourth level is when students are allowed to have group discussions about what they have learned—the retention increases to a 50 percent rate. The fifth level is called "practice by doing" and represents a retention rate of 75 percent. Practice by doing occurs when the child is asked to duplicate all the steps to a lesson. Finally, the sixth level, "teaching others" about what they have learned, represents our highest rate, or a 90 percent retention rate adapted from the NTL Institute's learning pyramid model [1960].

A student's interests, learning styles, abilities, and multiple intelligences will vary, and as such, so should the learning percentages of the Pyramid of Learning.

Brain Gains #79

If you want to create lessons that are boring and quickly forgotten, then use rote memorization. If you want students to have greater long-term storage, then use elaborative rehearsal.

First, Last, and Finally, the Primacy Effect

Once more, students will remember material that is introduced first and last, and frequently not the middle. Brain scientists call this the primacy/regency effect. For example, over a period of 20 minutes, the downtime is about 10 percent of the total time, or two minutes. In other words, as the learning episode decreases, the downtime decreases faster than the prime times, which is why teachers need to keep the learning episodes short and meaningful.

Therefore, teaching two 20-minute lessons causes 20 percent more prime time, or about 36 percent out of one 40-minute lesson. At 80 minutes, prime time decreases to 50 minutes, and total downtime is 30 minutes, and the percentage of total time is 38 percent. The bottom line is that more retention occurs when a lesson is shorter and meaningful. Perhaps this is one reason why block scheduling (e.g., 80-minute classes) would be problematic for students who have difficulty with on-task behavior.

Brain Gains #80

The first items of new information are within working memory or functional capacity, so they command our attention and are likely to be retained in semantic memory (i.e., verbal). Conversely, "information that is taught later, however, exceeds the working memory capacity and is lost. Further, as the learning episodes conclude, items in working memory are sorted or chunked to allow for additional processing of the arriving final items, which likely are held in working memory and will decay unless further rehearsed" (Gazzaniga, 2008).

Prime- and Downtimes

Parents should take heed of prime- and downtimes with homework. Parents need to learn their child's prime and down homework times, particularly with the length of their homework period. For example, parents should use the 10-minute homework rule, beginning with first graders working on homework for 10 minutes, then second grade for 20 minutes, and so on (National Education Association, n.d.).

Brain Gains #81

Using a planner helps keep the brain organized!

Brain Gains #82

At least 117 different molecules play a role when neurons create a memory.

7
Reading

Reading begins when information is taken into the brain in the form of letters and words, the information is sent to the occipital lobe, or vision center, then decoded on the left side of the brain or the angular gyros. The angular gyros divide the word into basic sounds (44 phonemes). This activity stimulates the language centers for auditory processing of the brain or left hemisphere. The sounds are interpreted and sent to the Wernicke (interpretation of words) and Broca's (speaking) areas for interpretation (mental dictionaries) and then sent to the frontal lobe for meaning.

For instance, take the word "dog." Again, the visual word "dog" is sent to the visual cortex located in the occipital lobe or in the back area of the brain. The word is decoded (interpreted) located on the left side of the brain in *D . . . O . . . G* or phonemes, where (left hemisphere—temporal lobe) auditory processing occurs. The auditory processing system sounds out the phonemes in the head or *duh . . . awh . . . guh*. Again, the two main areas, Broca's and Wernicke's areas, supply information about the word to our mental storage areas. The frontal lobe integrates the word into meaning: a furry animal that barks, or "dog."

—*David Sousa, 2005*

Learning how to read could be the most important and challenging school experience for some children, particularly boys. For example, a typical parent might ask why her seven-year-old son is having problems with reading comprehension, yet he possesses a high ability to read orally with speed, accuracy, and expression. In fact, it is assumed that high reading fluency and reading comprehension should go hand in hand. However, reading comprehension is a skill of complex combinations—far beyond merely the pronunciation of a word, which many parents tend to focus on.

In truth, high reading fluency can become a detriment for many children when they must read silently because they have a tendency to skip words, which could affect reading comprehension. Nevertheless, although teachers and parents understand that reading is a very complicated task for the brain, teaching reading is often met with a great deal of consternation because it is so difficult for some beginning readers.

Brain Gains #83

"In both referred and research-identified samples, greater numbers of males with reading problems have typically been reported. For example, in a recent review of sex differences in reading disability, Rutter et al. (2004) reported the gender ratios in four independent epidemiological studies in which the samples had been ascertained using research criteria. In all four of the studies, significantly more males than females with reading disabilities were reported. Moreover, gender ratios for reading difficulties are greater in more severely affected samples" (Hawke et al., 2009).

A quick review of the different parts of the brain responsible for reading might explain why learning to read is so challenging. First, there is the visual cortex that is responsible for deciphering images, such as letters, words, and so on. A second area is the auditory cortex, which focuses on sounds or long and short vowels. Add in Broca's and Wernicke's brain regions, which are crucial for processing language and/or communication, such as oral reading and listening comprehension, and we understand some of the difficulties with learning to read.

Still, the real work begins for the child when he is now required to develop the skills that must integrate all these brain processes to actually read. This includes phonology or phonemic awareness, alphabet principles, vocabulary, text comprehension, and, of course, fluency.

Brain Gains #84

One basic strategy reading specialists suggest for facilitating better reading comprehension is the use of a "paper slider." A slider is an index card with a center slit that allows the child to isolate each sentence read. By isolating the word or sentence, the reader can actively stimulate the brain area or visual cortex, which could then support better reading comprehension. In addition, the slider also teaches the child to "chunk" words rather than to read them singularly. Once more, research shows that the brain remembers the first and last letters of a word (i.e., the primacy/recency effect) and often forgets or skips over the middle. Further, "chunking" could help your child's reading fluency because it activates working memory and retention. (Note to reader: Please review chapter six, "Memory," for additional information concerning chunking and the primacy/recency effect.

Once again, choral reading, echo reading, guided reading, and reader's theater are all excellent reading strategies that stimulate the auditory cortex and allow greater fluency and comprehension with readers.

Brain Gains #85

"Choral reading is an interpretive reading of text, often poetry or songs, by a group of voices. Students may read individual lines or stanzas alone, in pairs, or in unison. Choral reading, sometimes called 'unison reading,' requires repeated readings of a particular passage, and it gives practice in oral reading.

"It is especially well suited to rhymes, poetry, and lyrics. As part of the activity, the teacher also reads to help set the pace, as well as model proper pronunciation. The poems or passages can be 'performed' for other students. Ultimately, though, enjoyment and learning should come out of the process of figuring out *how* to perform the poem rather than the performance itself" (American Master for Teachers, n.d.).

Brain Gains #86

Please Google *Dr. David Sortino: Increasing Reading Fluency with Beginning Readers.*

"'Guided reading' is a strategy in which the teacher mentors a child or a small group through the reading of a selection, drawing them into an exploration of the context, the content, and the words. Helping students understand the meaning of a reading passage, book, or novel is the key. The small group, ideally no more than six, should be comprised of students who are on the same level and need further work in similar reading areas.

"'Reader's theater' allows students to take any piece of literature, analyze it, and adapt it into a script. Originally popular in college courses, reader's theater is used as a fun, convenient, and effective way to create interest in reading among young children" (American Master for Teachers, n.d.).

Also, all strategies listed here reinforce Broca's and Wernicke's regions of the brain, causing the child to listen and then speak the material he has just heard. Moreover, this strategy stimulates the brain's hippocampus (i.e., consolidation of information from short-term to long-term memory and spatial navigation), attaching (i.e., bonding) a positive personal experience to reading, which could induce greater memory consolidation.

Even the cerebellum, our most primitive part of the brain and seat of the sensory-motor area of the brain (i.e., kinesthetic), can be stimulated by having the child drag his finger over the words he is reading. Again, Montessori used this approach with sandpaper letters to teach the alphabet to beginning readers. Bottom line—reading fluency and comprehension is more than just an acquired skill. In fact, it is an essential part of acquiring a successful reading identity that can be embraced for years to come.

Brain Gains #87

There is NO specific area of the brain that specializes in reading (Sousa, 2006).

For the most part, reading is a relatively new activity for the brain because it was not a prerequisite for our survival. In other words, we spoke before we read, and as such, in the evolutionary scheme of things, reading requires multiple brain areas to function.

The first encounter your child will have with reading is usually with his eyes, although studies encourage parents to begin reading to infants (i.e., auditory), and as they mature, the parents should read while pointing to the words in the story, including any illustrations that support the story.

Brain Gains #88

Please Google *Dr. David Sortino: Developmental Delays and School Readiness*.

Brain Gains #89

"When should you have your child's eyes examined? Children should have their first comprehensive eye exam at six months of age. After six months, parents should have a child's eyes examined at age three and just before they enter the first grade—at about age five or six. School-aged children should have an eye exam at least every two years if no vision correction is required. Children who need eyeglasses or contact lenses should be examined annually or as recommended by your eye doctor" (Heiting, 2019).

Brain Gains #90

"Studies have also shown that children who were read to as newborns have a larger vocabulary, as well as more advanced mathematical skills, than other kids their age. There's also a direct link between how many words a baby hears each day and her language skills. One study found that babies whose parents spoke to them a lot scored higher on standardized tests when they reached age three than children whose parents weren't as verbal" (Diproperzio, 2019).

Furthermore, learning to read successfully requires critical neural systems to work together to help the brain decode abstract symbols into meaningful language.

Nevertheless, if the child's auditory processing ability is weak (e.g., decoding or sounding out the letters and/or words), his auditory center will call on the brain's visual center to represent the letters or words to ensure they are being read correctly. If difficulties still persist, the frontal lobe will ask for another visual scan or return the child to auditory processing. All these actions occur within a fraction of a second! This process may seem sequential or linear, but the process is actually bidirectional or parallel with multiple phonemes processed simultaneously (Sousa, 2006).

Additionally, working memory plays a large part as to whether or not the beginning reader will remember word sounds. This is why struggling readers must be taught using multiple modalities. Montessori and Waldorf schools recognize that beginning readers need multiple modalities (e.g., art- or kinesthetic-centered curriculums) that can help children to learn how to read successfully.

Also, there will be several skill areas associated with the brain and reading mastery. The first is "phonetic awareness" or the ability to hear and manipulate the sounds in spoken words and the understanding that spoken words and syllables are made up of sequences of speech sounds (Yopp, 1992).

In addition, phonemic awareness means the child can distinguish between "bat" and "pat," or "bat" and "bet." Further, the child needs to be able to isolate each sound in order from first to last, as well as be able to segment words into different phonemes (e.g., reading part to whole, rather than whole to part).

Another skill area occurs when our 26-letter alphabet asks the child to understand that words are made up of phonemes, which represent letters. Through practice, our brains can match up a few letters to understand the word, or what brain scientists refer to as chunking or patterning. When the child reads the word "student," he does not read each letter individually but reads the entire word.

Brain Gains #91

Children four years old and younger can chunk no more than three letters, with an average of two letters; between ages five and 14, the average is five, and the maximum is seven. Gifted readers have the advantage or the ability to sight-read (i.e., chunk) and transfer the word into long-term storage and then retrieve the word from memory (Miller, 1956; Cowan, 2001).

Young children who have reading difficulties attempt to chunk, but the word never makes it into long-term storage, which is why such children need to be taught "phonetically" or employ other teaching modalities.

Vocabulary, another essential component, occurs when the child builds a mental dictionary to recognize words. The reason for the development of a mental vocabulary is that children learn and develop vocabulary by listening and speaking to adults. In addition, vocabulary development comes in many forms, such as through enriched reading exercises, which is why parents need to talk and/or read to their child, making such acts pleasant and the relationship positively oriented.

Furthermore, when parents and teachers focus on enrichment, the brain's hippocampus, the seat of emotional relationships, is stimulated, which allows the child not only to form a positive relationship (i.e., bonding) with the child's reading intelligence, but also to stimulate the child's higher centers of the brain (i.e., frontal lobes), causing greater memory consolidation and comprehension.

"Fluency is the ability to read like you speak. Reading fluency is made up of at least three key elements: accurate reading of connected text, at a conversational rate, and with appropriate prosody or expression. Non-fluent readers suffer in at least one of these aspects of reading: They make many mistakes, they read slowly, and/or they don't read with appropriate expression and phrasing" (Read Naturally, n.d.).

Brain Gains #92

For students who are 11 and older, a speed-reading class could be beneficial for some because it teaches them to chunk, which can increase reading fluency. In a word, children with high fluency read more rapidly, preventing the working memory from being distracted (i.e., visual/auditory), and leading to greater reading comprehension.

The last area is "text comprehension," or the ability to understand word meaning through contextual cues, such as inferences, or understanding the difference between fact and fiction, and so on. Again, parents and teachers can stimulate text comprehension through extensive enrichment activities.

Brain Gains #93

Please Google *Dr. David Sortino: How Many Books Do You Have in Your Home?*

There are many problems that can affect your child's reading ability, particularly when the child's visual center works faster than the child's auditory center. For instance, a major problem can occur when the child's eyes scan words but the auditory center is too slow to sound out the word. The end result is that the child not only stumbles over the sounds to pronounce the words, but since working memory is so temporary, they also consistently have problems remembering how to sound out the phonemes.

Brain Gains #94

"Male brains utilize nearly seven times more gray matter for activity, while female brains utilize nearly ten times more white matter. What does this mean? Gray matter areas of the brain are localized. They are information- and action-processing centers in splotches in a specific area of the brain. This can translate to a kind of tunnel vision when they are doing something.

"Once they are deeply engaged in a task or game, they may not demonstrate much sensitivity to other people or their surroundings. White matter is the networking grid that connects the brain's gray matter and other processing centers with one another. This profound brain-processing difference is probably one reason you may have noticed that girls tend to more quickly transition between tasks than boys do. The gray-white matter difference may explain why, in adulthood, females are great multitaskers, while men excel in highly task-focused projects" (Jantz, 2014).

Again, a Montessori curriculum technique will often create sandpaper letters. Thus, children could simultaneously touch (i.e., kinesthetic) and say the phonemes or alphabet letters as a way to stimulate the brain's cerebellum or kinesthetic and linguistic intelligences at the same time. Bottom line: This method was used successfully to produce a more intense working-memory experience, which could support greater long-term memory.

Other problems that can affect a child's reading skills have to do with phonological delays and/or phonological disorders. Phonological delay is employed when a child has patterns of speech that are more typical of a younger child. The sound system is developing normally, but at a much slower rate than expected. Phonological disorders involve some delays but also the use of phonological processes that are atypical, inconsistent, or not following the expected pattern of phonological development. This is likely to make the child's pronunciation less clear, and his avoidance of reading may be more persistent and require the support of a reading specialist.

Brain Gains #95

"Phonological disorder is often divided into three categories, based on the cause of the disorder. One cause is structural problems, or abnormalities in the areas necessary for speech sound production, such as the tongue or the roof of the mouth. These abnormalities make it difficult for children to produce certain sounds, and in some cases, they make it impossible for a child to produce the sounds at all.

"The structural problem causing the phonological disorder generally needs to be treated before the child goes into language therapy. This therapy is especially useful because, in many of these cases, correction of the structural problem results in correction of the speech-sound problem.

"The second category of phonological disorder are problems caused by neurological problems or abnormalities. This category includes problems with the muscles of the mouth that do not allow the child sufficient fine motor control over the muscles to produce all speech sounds. The third category of phonological disorder is of an unknown cause. This is sometimes called 'developmental phonological disorder.'

"Although the cause is not known, there is much speculation. Possible causes include slight brain abnormalities, causes rooted in the child's environment, and immature development of the neurological system. As of 2002, there is research pointing to all of these factors, but no definitive cause has been found" (Encyclopedia of Mental Disorders, 2019).

In addition, there are the actual rare but occasional physical disabilities, leading to lack of reading fluency. Some children may suffer from "lesions" in the left side of the brain or temporal lobe, causing difficulty with reading. "Word blindness" can also occur when the child with normal eyesight lacks the ability to read words caused by congenital defects to the word processing areas.

Other causes of poor reading skills are described as "nonlinguistic causes." For instance, a child may not be able to detect and decipher sounds presented in quick succession caused by weak auditory processing. Still others lack the habit to hear differences in sound frequency (i.e., the Wernicke area).

The auditory deficits affect the ability to discriminate tone and pitch in speech, which could affect how the child sounds out different phonemes. Lastly, even a child's lack of ability to detect tones within a noisy background can cause reading difficulties, particularly within the auditory centers of the brain.

One of the least discussed concerns with reading has to do with motor coordination and the brain's cerebellum. For instance, how the child's eyes move across a page can play a significant role in reading, writing, spelling, and so on.

Brain Gains #96

Please Google *Dr. David Sortino: Intelligence and the Lost Art of Cursive Writing.*

"Developmental dyslexia" can also present significant reading problems, such as the child experiencing unexpected difficulty in learning to read, despite adequate intelligence, supportive environments, and normal sensory ability. Developmental dyslexia is a spectrum disorder (i.e., a range of disabilities) varying from mild to severe. Neuroimaging studies have established that there are significant differences in the way normal and dyslexic brains respond to specific spoken and written language tasks.

Brain Gains #97

"Developmental dyslexia is characterized by difficulties with accurate and/or fluent word recognition and by poor spelling and decoding abilities. These difficulties typically result from a deficit in the phonological component of language that is often unexpected in relation to other cognitive abilities and the provision of effective classroom instruction. Secondary consequences may include problems in reading comprehension and reduced reading experience that can impede growth of vocabulary and background knowledge" (International Dyslexia Association, n.d.).

Furthermore, there is strong evidence that these differences may weaken with appropriate instructional interventions (Shaywitz, 2003). To sum up, reading is an unnatural act for most children, and the wise parent or teacher will take the time to research strategies and techniques to help him master this essential but very difficult task.

For instance, one successful reading program for struggling readers is called Fast ForWord, developed by Scientific Learning Associates. This program has shown to successfully offer support to both teachers and parents to help readers of all ages and levels achieve reading proficiency. The strength of Fast ForWord is that parents can implement the computerized program at home and teachers can access it in the classroom.

Most important, Fast ForWord has improved the students' reading brains and learning at all grade levels, among all genders, including all socioeconomic levels. The rate of improvement is much greater than those of other programs such as Science Research Associates (SRA).

Further, the Fast ForWord program takes a direct approach to the child's critical reading brain areas. For example, Fast ForWord stimulates the brain's "prime reading areas" as well as increases the student's ability to perform basic cognitive functions essential to reading and learning. Moreover, Fast ForWord has shown to increase memory, attention, processing, and sequencing skills of students at all grade levels.

A major component associated with reading mastery and a strength of the Fast ForWord program is the ability to stimulate the student's working memory (i.e., the ability to chunk phonemes, letters, etc., into words) and has improved long-term memory or the ability for the student to retrieve information necessary for reading proficiency and comprehension.

Besides, Fast ForWord recognizes the brain's plasticity (i.e., ability to develop) by exercising the brain's reading processing centers through intensive adaptive exercises, so actual physical changes can occur in the child's reading brain, another essential ingredient for successful reading and learning potential.

Another excellent tool to support teachers and parents associated with the Fast ForWord program is called the "Reading Assistant." This program builds brain fitness through intensive reading practice, using speech verification technology to act as a tutor, providing one-to-one guided oral reading support.

A four-year Reading Assistant study conducted in the Dallas ISD showed struggling students made significant improvement on their text assessment of knowledge and skills (TAKS), narrowing the achievement gap by 25 percent. Another study of the Louisiana Educational Assessment Program (LEAP) and the Integrated Louisiana Educational Assessment Program (ILEAP) for Fast ForWord users showed that, over a two-year period, the number of fourth graders scoring "Basic" or above in reading increased from 19 to 81 percent, and the number scoring "Basic" or above in math increased from 9 to 71 percent!

Finally, the Fast ForWord program also includes the Scientific Learning Progress Tracker, which uses an online data analysis and reporting tool that enables educators to monitor individual, classroom, and school or district performance of students. Educators get clear, detailed, action-oriented information showing student progress over a period of time as related to specific reading and cognitive areas that are necessary components for reading mastery.

Brain Gains #98

For further information, please Google *Fast Forward and the Scientific Learning Process.*

Listed here is a left/right brain assessment that parents and teachers can employ with students to determine the effect hemispheric dominance could have on your student's reading brain. Although research has been conflicted as to whether individuals are left-brain or right-brain dominant, educators recognize that the two sides of the brain often play a specialized role in reading and writing.

That is, the right side of the brain represents the visual or spatial, and the left side of the brain, the verbal and linear. In my opinion, identifying whether or not your student displays left- or right-brain dominance could be another link to support more effective reading and writing skills as well as add to the *Brain Gains/Learning Coach* concept.

For additional information about teaching to the left and right sides of students' brains, please see chapter 10, "Left/Right-Brain Teaching."

8

Learning Styles

Many people prefer to learn in ways that are different from how other people of the same class, grade, age, nationality, race, culture, or religion prefer to learn. How people prefer to learn is their learning style preference. Although some gifted students can learn proficiently without using their learning style preferences, low achievers perform significantly better when they capitalize on their preferences. A decade of research demonstrates that both low and average achievers earn higher scores on standardized achievement tests and attitude tests when taught through their learning style preferences.

—Rita Dunn, How to Implement and Supervise a Learning Style Program

1. ACTIVE AND REFLECTIVE LEARNERS

"'Let's try it out and see how it works' is the 'active learner's' phrase; 'let's think it through first' is the 'reflective learner's' response. Active learners are the opposite of reflective learners, who tend to like group work because they can interact and use their interpersonal and verbal intelligence" (Felder & Solomon, 2008).

Brain Gains #99

"'Interpersonal intelligence' reflects an ability to recognize and understand other people's moods, desires, motivations, and intentions. Verbal-linguistic intelligence—along with logical-mathematical intelligence—is often associated with doing well in school. It involves the ability to use words effectively for reading, writing, listening, and speaking. The poet has been described as the epitome of verbal-linguistic intelligence" (Edutopia, 2016).

On the other hand, reflective learners prefer working alone or in the intrapersonal world of multiple intelligence. Sitting through a class lecture and not being able to do anything physical besides taking notes is difficult for both learning style types, yet particularly difficult for active learners. Therefore, let the active learner work with a partner, taking turns teaching one another, or better yet, let them research a topic of their choice and present it to the class.

Brain Gains #100: The Pyramid of Learning

Verbal Processing = Lecture = 5%

Verbal Processing = Reading = 10%

Verbal and Visual Processing = Demonstration = 30%

Verbal and Visual Processing = Discussion Group = 50%

Doing = Practice by Doing = 75%

Doing = Teach Others/Immediate Use of Learning = 90%

(Taylor and Trott, 1991)

The average retention rate after 24 hours shows that students will only remember 5 percent of a lecture. Interestingly, verbal processing is the major approach in most high school classes. The second level, also associated with verbal processing, is reading, with a 10 percent retention rate. The third level combines verbal and visual processing, or the audio-visual, and has a 30 percent retention rate.

The fourth level is when students are allowed to have group discussions about what they have learned—the retention increases to a 50 percent rate. The fifth level is called "practice by doing" and represents a retention rate of 75 percent. Practice by doing occurs when the child is asked to duplicate all the steps to a lesson. Finally, the sixth level, "teaching others" about what they have learned, represents our highest rate, or a 90 percent retention rate.

Since a student's interests, learning styles, abilities, and multiple intelligence will vary, so should the learning percentages of the Pyramid of Learning.

A major problem with reflective learners is that, as children, they can be very deliberate in how they learn and think. Therefore, parents and teachers often believe they are not only procrastinating but are also not "school intelligent." Some parents even suggest that these children may have a "learning disability"!

Reflective learners need time to process information because they tend to digest every word that you say. They dwell on every thought, examining every possible angle. Nevertheless, give them time and they could come up with a brilliant answer! Moreover, such children are often "spatial learners" and see the world "whole-to-part." As a result, they may have difficulties as an early reader, sequencing conversations and class activities and discussions, which is why they seem to dwell on every word and every action.

Brain Gains #101

"The capacity to sequence information is central to human performance. Sequencing ability forms the foundation stone for higher order cognition related to language and goal-directed planning. Information related to the order of items, their timing, chunking and hierarchical organization are important aspects in sequencing" (Savalia, Shukla, and Bapi, 2016).

Active learners have a tendency to skip over important points and, as a result, may not get the entire meaning of the lesson or what is being said. Active learners often sit in the front of the class and are the first to raise their hands, regardless of whether they know the entire answer. In class, they can be weak note takers and often lose track of class lectures because when they are bored they will often engage other students to help them deal with their boredom.

On the other hand, reflective learners are often slow at note taking because they want to write down everything you say. Parents can buy them a tape recorder, and they can, with the teacher's permission, tape the class lecture.

Brain Gains #102

"Cognitive abilities are brain-based skills that we need to carry out any task from the simplest to the most complex. They have more to do with the mechanisms of how we learn, remember, problem-solve, and pay attention, rather than with any actual knowledge. For instance, answering the telephone involves perception (hearing the ring tone), decision making (answering or not), motor skills (lifting the receiver), language skills (talking and understanding language), social skills—interpreting tone of voice and interacting properly with another human being" (Michelon, 2006).

In addition, there will be those students who fall in the middle: active sometimes and reflective depending on the subject matter. A student's preference for one category or for the other may vary from weak to strong. A balance of the two is desirable. If the student always acts before reflecting, he can jump into things prematurely and experience confusion. Conversely, if he spends too much time reflecting on a particular subject, he may lose track of the lesson and never get anything done.

How Active Learners Can Help Themselves

Active learners should try to study in a group or teach the material to others. (Note: Please see the entry in the Appendix on the Pyramid of Learning.) Also, outlining information on a whiteboard could satisfy the need to be physical or kinesthetic. On tests, they can try to predict test questions or create game show questions and answers. Remember, they will learn best if they do something physical with it.

Brain Gains #103

Eat a good breakfast the morning of the test. Studies show that students who drink an eight-ounce glass of water combined with dried fruit increased their success test rate by 35 percent when compared to students who did not drink water or consume dried fruit. Remember: The brain requires three basic ingredients to function: fructose, water, and oxygen!

Also, if the active learner is in a class that allows little or no class time for discussion or problem-solving activities, they could try to compensate for this limited opportunity for class discussion with a study group with members taking turns explaining different topics or ideas to one another.

Further, a good test-taking strategy is for active learners to work with others and to guess what will be asked on the test. Bottom line: Active learners seem to retain information better if they find ways to do something with it.

How Reflective Learners Can Help Themselves

If your child is a reflective learner who attends classes that allow little or no class time for discussion of new information, they should try to compensate for this lack with the study skills trick that follows.

Brain Gain Notes #104

Here is how one student connected his professor's class lectures with test questions.

If you attended the lecture and paid attention, you would (or should!) note that he often used many verbal cues about probable exam material. Material he seemed to lecture on and on about had to be important (and indeed it was!). Or, more often than not, he would directly tell you this is an "important topic" that is "worth knowing."

All the smart students went to every class, paid attention, and took note of topics he deemed "worth knowing." Come midterm time, the student hadn't really done the "required" readings, but as most of them figured out, it was the lecture component that the teacher really wanted them to know, not just some obscure passage that had never been mentioned in class (unlike some other psychology courses). It also helped that the professor gave them the exact format of the exam: some multiple choice, some definitions, a few short answers, and one long essay question. Knowing this, the student could tailor their studying accordingly.

He went through all the lecture notes in detail, made sure he knew all the definitions, and tried to compare and contrast various psycho-perspectives, as the professor hinted at. He generated some of his own exam questions, and boy, was he glad, because some of them showed up on the exam! So, using the professor's verbal cues and hints, he predicted what the exam questions might be like, and lo and behold, there they were, in front of his eyes on exam day. He had never been so glad he tried out this method. It's a great exam prep strategy—try it yourself for your next exam! I can almost guarantee you will do better (*Study Skills Tips*, 2010).

The moral of the story is students should never just read or memorize the material; instead, they should stop periodically to review what they have read and think of possible questions or applications. Also, students might find it helpful to write short summaries of readings or class notes in their own words. Doing so may take extra time, but this will enable the student to retain the material more effectively.

For younger children, you can read the summaries to your child and then have the child explain what you have just read in their own words.

Exercise #1: Think of a time when your child might have demonstrated an active learning style.

Exercise #2: Think of a time when your child might have demonstrated a reflective learning style.

2. SENSING AND INTUITIVE LEARNERS

"Sensing learners" tend to like learning facts because, as the word implies, a sensing learning style is the ability to be able to "learn with one's senses," which can often be concrete and predictable. Sensing learners usually do well on tests that are short answer, true/false, and multiple choice.

Brain Gains #105

The multiple-choice format is commonly used in testing because the exams are relatively easy to grade, and the questions effectively evaluate students' knowledge of facts and understanding of concepts. Unlike multiple choice tests, true-false answers should not be changed unless one is absolutely sure of the answer. If one is not sure, it is best to stick with the original impulse and write an explanation in the margin of the test.

On the other hand, "intuitive learners" often prefer discovering possibilities and relationships and do well on long answer or essay tests. Moreover, sensory learners often like solving problems by well-established methods and dislike complications and surprises.

Brain Gains #106

"The sensory learning style, also known as the VAK, uses the three main sensory receivers: visual, auditory, and kinesthetic. Students often prefer one style of learning, which defines the best way for that student to learn new information. Sensory learning styles indicate that *35 percent of people are mainly visual learners, 25 percent are auditory learners, and 40 percent are kinesthetic learners*" (Wanamaker, 2016).

Brain Gains #107

"Spatial ability includes spatial judgment and the ability to visualize things. Think of people who think in pictures, can solve the Rubik's Cube game very quickly, or can spot tiny differences between seemingly identical pictures" ("Multiple Intelligences," n.d.).

Intuitive learners like innovation and dislike repetition. Sensory learners are more likely than intuitive learners to resent being tested on material that has not been explicitly covered in class. Sensory learners tend to be patient with details and are good at memorizing facts and using hands-on (i.e., science) work. Intuitive learners may be better at grasping new concepts or ideas and can be more comfortable than sensory learners with abstractions and mathematical formulations. Ask an intuitive learner how he got the answer, and he may say: "I just know it!"

Brain Gains #108

"'Intuition,' argues Gerd Gigerenzer, a director at the Max Planck Institute for Human Development, 'is less about suddenly "knowing" the right answer and more about instinctively understanding what information is unimportant and can thus be discarded.'

"Gigerenzer, author of the book *Gut Feelings: The Intelligence of the Unconscious*, says that he is both intuitive and rational. 'In my scientific work, I have hunches. I can't explain always why I think a certain path is the right way, but I need to trust it and go ahead. I also have the ability to check these hunches and find out what they are about. That's the science part. Now, in private life, I rely on instinct. For instance, when I first met my wife, I didn't do computations. Nor did she'" (Kasanoff, 2017).

Sensory learners tend to be more practical and careful than intuitive learners. Intuitive learners tend to work faster and be more innovative than sensory learners, so teachers need to allow intuitive learners the opportunity for greater creativity. Sensory learners don't like courses/lessons that have no apparent connection to the real world; intuitive learners don't like plug-and-chug lessons/courses that involve a lot of memorization and routine calculations.

Like active and reflective learners, everybody is a sensory learner sometimes and an intuitive learner at other times. A preference for one or the other may be strong, moderate, or mild. To be an effective learner and problem solver, sensory or intuitive learners need to be able to function in both worlds. If an intuitive learner overemphasizes intuition, he may miss important details or make careless mistakes in calculation or hands-on work. If a sensory learner overemphasizes sensing, he may rely too much on memorization and familiar methods and not concentrate enough on understanding and innovative thinking.

How Sensory Learners Can Help Themselves

Sensory learners can help themselves when they are trying to remember and understand information, to see how it connects to the real world. If you are in a middle school or high school class where the material is abstract and/or theoretical, you may have difficulty. Ask your teacher for *specific examples* of concepts and procedures, and find out how other concepts apply in practice. If the teacher does not provide enough facts or specifics, refer to your class text or other references or try brainstorming with friends or classmates (Felder and Solomon, 2008).

Brain Gains #109

"Sensory processing disorder is characterized by difficulties in accurately processing a range of sensory information, such as touch, sound, and smell. It can be tricky for parents and teachers to manage due to the two opposite ways it can manifest—hypersensitivity and hyposensitivity" (Dean, 2015).

How Intuitive Learners Can Help Themselves

Intuitive learners often prefer discovering possibilities and relationships, and they are more comfortable with abstractions. They work faster and with more innovation, hating drill-and-kill assignments. Further, they can be prone to making careless mistakes, so they need to read assignments more than once. Again, this learner will often give you the answer, and when you ask how they got the answer, they will smile and say, "I just know it." We need to respect this type of learner because their knowledge comes from observations connected to emotions. In their own way, they have been observing life at an early age. They may appear to act like space cadets, but internally, they have been processing and understanding how everything is interconnected. In the "Multiple Intelligence World," they could be defined as spatial learners.

Brain Gains #110

"Intuitive knowledge is complex. It should not be taken for granted or otherwise discounted. In fact, teachers should devote more time and energy to understanding and improving this knowledge base. All teachers learn from experience, but that doesn't guarantee that what they've learned is correct. To learn more about that intuitive knowledge, the author suggests that instructors need to become more reflective and more aware of their responses, especially those responses not particularly effective. Then they need to talk with colleagues, finding out how others respond to a particular kind of situation. And sometimes busy instructors just need to be still. They need to stop those busy minds that would like to force intuition into the rational mold. 'Quiet contemplation rather than intense concentration may be more likely to yield up a novel solution to an instructional dilemma'" (Weimer, 2013).

Few classes in elementary school are aimed at intuitive learners because students are being taught skill development. However, as they move to middle and high school, where abstract thinking and conceptualization is required, the intuitive learner will feel more comfortable, if their academic skills can support his learning style.

Moreover, if your child is an intuitive learner and he happens to be in a class that deals primarily with memorization and rote learning, he may have problems with boredom and focus. Intuitive learners should ask the teacher for examples that link the facts or try to discover the connections themselves. In addition, they may be prone to careless mistakes on tests because they are impatient with details and do not like repetition.

Exercise #3: Think of a time when your child/student might have been a sensing learner.

Exercise #4: Think of a time when your child/student might have been an intuitive learner.

3. VISUAL AND VERBAL LEARNERS

"Visual learners" remember best when they can visualize assignments and/or learning paradigms as pictures, diagrams, flow charts, timelines, films, and demonstrations. Conversely, verbal learners learn best when the material is presented verbally or orally. However, verbal learners get more out of words that are written or spoken to support explanations.

Visual learners are relatives to Howard Gardner's (multiple intelligence) spatial intelligence learners, who need to visualize ideas or concepts to learn most effectively.

Conversely, verbal learners must always communicate their ideas orally and almost always are the first ones to raise their hands to respond in a class discussion, very much like our active learner.

On the other hand, visual learners often have a far-off look as if they were in another world, but all they are really doing is trying to see the entire picture or spatially. Verbal learners can follow a conversation from beginning to end and often do well in classes that allow for open discussions. Visual learners see and learn whole-to-part, which is why some are often early readers since they can sight-read rather than read phonemically or part-to-whole.

Brain Gains #111

Verbal/linguistic intelligence (sensitive to the meaning and order of words as in a poet): Use activities that involve hearing (intrapersonal intelligence is the ability involving introspection and self-reflective capacities). This refers to having a deep understanding of one's own strengths/weaknesses and predicting one's own reactions. Think of someone who is really good at setting and achieving self-goals based on an understanding of what he/she can accomplish, listening, impromptu or formal speaking, tongue twisters, humor, oral or silent reading, documentation, creative writing, spelling, journaling, and poetry.

Verbal learners would rather explain problems first in steps to others, and they do well in a lecture format in high school and college. Visual learners have been known to move slowly in elementary school because of the emphasis on drill but excel in middle and high school as late bloomers because they are now required to think abstractly. Moreover, it is critical that they develop good study skills for classroom success to take place.

How Verbal Learners Can Help Themselves

Have your child write summaries or outlines of course material in his own words and have him work in groups. He will understand material by hearing classmates' explanations and even more when the student or teacher explains or teaches the information to others. Have your child record lectures or use reading tapes for greater clarity and, for fun, practice play reading or simply sing songs.

Brain Gains #112

In order to get the most out of studying, you will want to capitalize on your strengths. For you, these strengths involve listening, speaking, and collaborating with others. A good place to start would simply be to read your notes out loud. This method allows you to hear the material and to process it through your own verbalization. Do this several times in order to make the most effective use of the strategy, as repetition is a key to retention of information. In addition, reading your textbook after each lesson and as you study will also help you to learn and to remember (Course Hero, 2018).

Brain Gains #113

Please see entry 1 in the Appendix about the Pyramid of Learning.

"Beyond these simple strategies, you can get a bit creative. Form study groups with your classmates in which you teach each other different chapters of the material. You can do this through Skype or other online resources. The ability to hear the lessons being taught to you will help you to process them" (Brighton College, 2018).

"Moreover, verbal learners thrive through the interpersonal connections offered in group work, as well. If you don't want to form a study group of classmates, perhaps you can teach the information to a friend or family member. That would also be beneficial. You could also find lectures of others discussing the material online if you'd like chances to listen to someone discussing the topic. Incorporate mnemonic devices like rhymes, acronyms, poems or other such verbal tools to help you remember certain phrases or concepts related to the assigned" (Brighton College, 2018).

Brain Gains #114

Please Google *Study Tips for Verbal Learners, Brighton College, 2018.*

How Visual Learners Can Help Themselves

If your child is a visual leaner, try to find diagrams, sketches, schematics, photographs, flow charts, timelines, films, or another visual representation and, of course, material that is also verbal. Once more, ask their teacher for visual examples and consult references to see any video tapes or whatever visual material is available. Prepare a concept map by listing key points, enclosing them in boxes, and drawing lines with arrows between concepts to show connections. Also, color-code notes with a highlighter so that everything relating to one topic is the same color ("Understanding Your Learning Style," n.d.).

Brain Gains #115

"If you use the visual style, you prefer using images, pictures, colors, and maps to organize information and communicate with others. You can easily visualize objects, plans and outcomes in your mind's eye. You also have a good spatial sense, which gives you a good sense of direction. You can easily find your way around using maps, and you rarely get lost. When you walk out of an elevator, you instinctively know which way to turn" (Learning Styles Online, 2019).

> Exercise #5: Think of a time when your child/student exhibited a visual learning style.
>
> Exercise #6: Think of a time when your child/student exhibited a verbal learning style.

4. SEQUENTIAL AND GLOBAL LEARNERS

Sequential learners think in linear steps, with each step following logically from the previous one, or by using an inductive process as in part-to-whole. Global learners like to learn in large jumps, absorbing material almost randomly without seeing connections, and then suddenly getting it (like spatial learners) as in whole-to-part or deductively. Sequential learners tend to follow logical sequential paths in finding solutions (Felder and Solomon, 2008).

Brain Gains #116

"You may get hung up on details when reading. You have to understand something before you move on. You might get frustrated easily with people who don't understand things as quickly as you do" (Fleming, 2019).

Global Learners

Global learners may be able to solve problems quickly or put ideas and concepts together in novel ways once they have grasped the big picture, but they may find it difficult explaining how they did it! Most people who read this description may conclude incorrectly that they are global learners since everyone has experienced bewilderment, followed by a sudden flash of understanding (Gutow, 2017).

Strong global learners who lack good sequential thinking abilities may have serious difficulties understanding information until they see the big picture. Further, even after they see the big picture, they may be unclear about the details of the subject, while sequential learners may know a lot about specific aspects of a subject, but may have difficulty showing the relationship between all parts.

How Sequential Learners Can Help Themselves

Most lessons are taught in a sequential manner, or step-by-step. However, if your student is a sequential learner and he has a teacher who jumps around from topic to topic or skips steps, he may have difficulty following and remembering. Have your student ask the teacher to review the unclear sequences or have your student listen to tapes of his class lectures.

When sequential learners are studying, they need to take the time to outline the class material in step-by-step order. They might also try to strengthen their global/abstract thinking skills by relating each new topic they study to concrete experiences of learning material. The more they can apply their learning, the better their understanding of the topic.

Brain Gains #117

You may get hung up on details when reading. You have to understand something before you move on. You might get frustrated easily with people who don't understand things as quickly as you do.

How Global Learners Can Help Themselves

Global learners need to see the big picture before they can master details, so have your student review chapters first to get an overview. They need to immerse themselves in individual subjects. For example, students who try to sight-read at an early age often drive parents and teachers crazy because they reject phonemic teaching. Again, an excellent program to improve reading fluency and comprehension, as well as auditory processing for such children, is called the Auditory Discrimination in Depth (ADD) Program.

Brain Gains #118

According to Patricia and Charles Lindamood, the developers of the ADD Program, the program approaches sound-symbol association from the opposite direction. First, the student explores the sound units of our language as sounds to hear, to see, and to feel their characteristics and then contrasts between them. The major premise of the ADD Program is that the auditory element of speech, sound, should not be separated from the more basic oral-motor activity that produces the sounds.

This emphasis links the succeeding level together as the program progresses from sound in isolation to sequences of sound in nonsense syllables to real words. They go on to say that the purpose of the basic experience is to develop the student's ability to consciously progress and use sensory cues from the ear, the eye, and the mouth. This three-way, cross-checking process sets up a self-monitoring system that is applicable in reading and spelling tasks in speech (Lindamood and Lindamood, 1975).

Brain Gains #119

"Global learners need to understand concepts before they start concentrating on the details. Endless facts tend to bore them, and they lose interest fast. They understand things better when they are introduced to them through short stories, illustrations, humor, or anecdotes. Global learners like to learn by being actively involved with information that is interesting and related to their lives. Children who prefer soft, light, and informal seating such as an easy chair, bed, or lying on the carpet are likely to be global learners. Having the TV on or music playing should not be cause for alarm. Such things actually help global learners by creating an environment that feels comfortable" ("Tips for Parents: Global vs. Analytic Learners," 2011).

How Global Learners Can Help Themselves

If your child is a global learner, it can be helpful for the parents or teacher to realize that he needs the big picture about the subject before he can master details. If the teacher plunges directly into new ideas/topics without bothering to explain how they relate to what the student already knows, it can cause problems for this type of learner.

Fortunately, there are steps parents/teachers can take to teach the global learner that may help him get the big picture more rapidly before he begins to study the first section of a chapter in a text. For example, have the global learner first skim through the entire chapter to get an overview. Although doing so may be time consuming initially, it may save him from experiencing confusion as he reads the individual parts.

Also, instead of spending a short time on every subject each night, your student might find it more productive to spend more time on a few subjects. Again, try to relate the subject to experiences or information he already knows. As a teacher or parent, help him see connections by consulting references. Eventually, he will understand the new material once he understands how it all connects to other topics, and it may enable him to apply the skill in ways that most sequential thinkers would never dream of.

- Exercise #7: Think of a time when your child exhibited a sequential learning style.
- Exercise #8: Think of a time when your child exhibited a global learning style.

9

Test-Taking

Tests are like death and taxes: If you do not prepare for them, they will get you. There are tests you take in school that will identify reading or math grade levels (STARR). There are tests that can get you a high school diploma called the CAHSEE (California High School Exit Exam) or the GED (Graduate Educational Development). There are tests that get you into college called SATs (Scholastic Aptitude Test) and tests to get you into graduate school called the GREs (Graduate Record Examination).

There is a whole battery of tests for teachers, lawyers, doctors, and psychologists to advance professionally. Then there are day-to-day tests such as a first date or your first day of high school. There are athletic tests or when you perform in a game situation and driver's education tests that can get you a driver's license.

The question that needs to be raised is that if tests are really going to be like death and taxes, we need to seriously teach our students how to take tests. Some teachers do it all the time, and it's called "teaching to test." One only needs to look at the number of private commercial test centers that dominate our world to see that test-taking skills is big business and something parents and students need to take more seriously. Therefore, it would make sense in a book about learning and intelligence to have a chapter that teaches and describes how to take tests for students. Here is only a sample of what they need to know to become effective test-takers.

—David Sortino, Tests—Like Death and Taxes

1. TEST-TAKING STRATEGIES

Strategy #1

The highest-performing test-taking technique is quizzing. This includes practice tests done by students on their own outside of class. Flashcards can be used to test recall or simply answering the same questions at the end of the textbook ranked the highest. Again, studies about learning and memory demonstrate the one process (the primacy-recency effect; see Brain Gains #120) students need to understand is that they will remember information at the beginning and end but forget the middle.

Brain Gains #120

"When we talk about the 'primacy effect' and the 'recency effect,' we are talking about the theory and application of the following: '. . . the *Primacy Effect* . . . you remember some things at the beginning of a list because it occurred first. There is the beginning, a long middle that blurs together, and now it is the end.' The *primacy effect* is the beginning. You remember it because that is where you started. The recency effect is the finish. You remember the end the best" (Morrison, 2015).

Strategy #2

Think about what the teacher considers most important. As a potential test-taker, imagine which part of the most recent material the teacher thinks is most important and make sure that you review that material. Finally, teachers have particular interests in the subjects they teach. Finding out what interests them could be a heads-up about what could be on their tests (see Brain Gains #62).

Strategy #3

Know key vocabulary, special terms, or formulas. You would not expect to buy food and then start to prepare a meal without knowing the recipe, let alone be able to read it.

Strategy #4

Form questions about the test material and see if you can answer them. The more you repeat this exercise, the more you are duplicating the test situation, and the more you attempt to duplicate the test material, the more confident you will feel. It is called "Teaching to Test."

Strategy #5

Lowering your anxiety level creates confidence. Lowering test anxiety begins with calming the emotional mid-brain or limbic system. When you calm the limbic system's right brain, you allow the left brain to take over, which can promote greater learning and even intelligence! For example, research shows that writing a letter to a friend for 15 to 30 minutes before taking a test has shown to eliminate test anxiety.

Brain Gains #121

"Tests and exams are stressful for many people. Students who 'choke' on an exam may perform less well than their knowledge base warrants. Such results can accumulate to generate reduced educational achievements and expectations. Studying young adults performing math tests, Ramirez and Beilock found that a brief intervention—writing about their anxiety about the upcoming exam—helped students to do better in the exam. Perhaps by acknowledging their fear, students were able to tame distracting emotions" (Ramirez and Beilock, 2011).

Brain Gains #122

Please Google *Dr. David Sortino: How Would Hemingway Deal with Test Anxiety?*

Strategy #6

Answer end-of-chapter questions. Again, this will reinforce the theory of beginnings, middles, and ends.

Strategy #7

Reread and review summaries, notes, outlines, and previous assignments.

Stategy #8

Compare your notes with a friend. First, it forces students to remember to pay attention and take notes in class. Second, every teacher wants to see their students succeed. The notes are often just another version of the test.

Strategy #9

Recite specific facts to yourself. You can do this when walking, driving a car, or riding a bike. For example, active or kinesthetic learners learn best when they integrate movement or communicate in small groups or teach the information to others.

Brain Gains #123

Please see the entry in the Appendix about the Pyramid of Learning.

Strategy #10

Practice working formulas and math problems. Learn the formula and the steps and you will succeed. Again, it is no different from cooking a meal—just follow the recipe.

Strategy #11

Before going to sleep, review test material. Sleep allows for hours of uninterrupted retention time.

Strategy #12

Get a good night's sleep. Understanding your body's circadian rhythms is critical to test-taking. Some of us are morning, afternoon, or evening people. If you stay on a schedule, you can regulate your rhythms. Adolescents are particular prone to poor sleep habits and need lots of sleep as well as a good diet. Care of your student's physical needs is often ignored but critically needed. Specifically, the ages of 15 to 16 is a period when most adolescents have the unhealthiest habits.

Brain Gains #124

"Short sleep duration, poor sleep quality, and late bedtimes are all associated with excess food intake, poor diet quality, and obesity in adolescents. Sleep, sedentary behavior, physical activity, and diet all interact and influence each other to ultimately impact health. A holistic approach to health (i.e., the whole day matters) targeting all of these behaviors 'synergistically' [the combined power of a group of things] is needed to optimize the impact of our interventions. Sleep is not a waste of time, and sleep hygiene is an important factor to consider in the prevention and treatment of obesity," (Chaput and Dutil, 2016).

Strategy #13

Eat a good breakfast the morning of the test. Studies show that students who drink an eight-ounce glass of water combined with dried fruit increased their success test rate by 35 percent when compared to students who did not drink water or consume dried fruit. The brain requires three basic ingredients to function: fructose, water, and oxygen.

Strategy #14

Again, another highly rated testing technique is called "distributed practice." Students usually mass their studies or cram. Instead, with distributed practice, students who practice over time were more effective in the tests that followed.

Brain Gains #125

Please Google *Dr. David Sortino: When Choosing Wrong Answers Can Be Right!*

Strategy #15

Elaborative and interrogation suggest that students should use "why" questions to facilitate higher learning with tests. Why questions produce explanations for facts. For instance, students should ask "Why is it true?" Studies show that, on factual tests, students who used elaborative interrogation answered about 72 percent questions correctly, compared to about 37 percent for other questions when they did not used elaborative interrogation. Also, why questions get students to think outside of the box, which is good for tapping in to the higher centers of the brain.

Strategy #16

Self-explanation is another excellent technique to improve test-taking and learning. For example, students can develop explanations for what they learn with such questions as: "What new information is provided here for greater learning?" and "How does it relate to what I already know?" Self-explanation is said to be beneficial for math tests, for logical reasoning, and for learning from narratives. With younger children, self-explanation can help with basic ideas such as learning numbers or for recognizing patterns. In addition, self-explanation is said to improve memory, comprehension, and problem-solving, which are all associated with the frontal lobe.

Strategy #17

What doesn't work? At the top of the list is "highlighting," which demonstrated little or no improved test performance. The problem is that highlighting zeros in on individual items rather than connecting across items, reducing a student's ability to actually think. At the very least, highlighting could be useful for self-tests. Thus, if you are going to highlight, then over-mark sparingly and try to connect the information to successful learning techniques as mentioned above.

Strategy #18

Another overrated learning technique is rereading, which is used by 84 percent of students. The researchers were skeptical that rereading would not increase comprehension because the results were based on levels of ability or knowledge. Still, it could work for recall, and better results occurred with the second rereading with diminishing returns thereafter.

2. THE DIFFERENT TYPES OF TESTS

You will be confronted with various types of tests during your time in school, such as objective tests, essay tests, and math tests, to name a few. If you make use of a few suggestions, understanding how to take these tests will be a valuable learning experience and tool for school and life success.

Strategy #1: Objective Tests

Objective tests generally require a short-answer response. There is usually only one right answer, and it is not an opinion. Objective tests frequently fall into one of four types: multiple choice, matching, short-answer, and true/false. Though there is no substitute for studying and learning material as the year progresses, here are some test-taking tips for each of these tests.

Strategy #2: Multiple-Choice Tests

Multiple-choice tests require the right answers from a number of possible choices. These tips can help you determine the correct answer:

1. First, read the entire question carefully. Circle words that you might be confused with or do not know.
2. Try to anticipate the answer before you look at the choices.
3. Read all the possible answers: They might all be correct, and the last choice might be "all of the above." Often, answers will appear in one question that you can use for other questions.
4. If you do not know which choice is correct, eliminate all the most obvious incorrect answers so that you can focus on the remaining choices. For example, mark the worst answer with a minus sign (–), mark the next best answer with a question mark, and mark the most likely answer with a plus (+). Then select the best answer, most likely the plus (+), from your choices.
5. Look for exact answers. Be aware of the words "always" or "never," as they are usually incorrect.
6. Look carefully at longer answers since it is often necessary to include more information to make a correct statement than a false one. Longer answers are often correct.

Strategy #3: Matching Tests

Matching tests usually give two lists of information and ask you to connect answers in some way. The following tips may help you:

1. Read the directions carefully. You may or may not be able to use an answer more than once.
2. Read the column with the most information, then match it with the column with the fewest words.
3. Use the process of elimination: Do the answers you know first, and cross them off.
4. Match the remaining choices.
5. Use your hunches. Research shows that the first answer that pops into your head is often correct.

Strategy #4: Short-Answer Tests

These tests require that you supply the answer. Try these tips:

1. If you do not know the answer, write down what you do know.
2. Guess—you have nothing to lose. Many tests grade you on what you get right.
3. Write alternate answers or hunches lightly, then place a question mark in the margin and come back to them later to choose the answer you think is best.

Strategy #5: True/False

True/false tests require you to make a judgment. These tips may help you make the correct choice.

1. For a statement to be true, it must be entirely true. If any part of a statement is false, then it is a false statement. Remember, you have a 50 percent chance of getting it right.
2. Be careful with statements that include words such as "all," "always," "only," or "never." They are often false.
3. If only part of the test is true/false, do those questions first. Once again, you may discover answers for other parts of the test.

Strategy #6: Taking the Test

1. Remember to read all the directions carefully. Be sure you understand whether to underline, circle, or write the word or letter. Ask your teacher if you are not sure.
2. Listen to all oral instructions. If the teacher reads the instructions on the page, you should reread them again.
3. Scan the test to see if some parts of the test are worth more points than others. Also, this will give you a general idea of what the test is about.
4. Plan your time so that you spend the greatest amount of time on the part that is worth the most points. If some questions carry more points than others, it is because the teacher feels those points are more important and possibly more difficult, so you want to spend more time on them.
5. If there is anything you do not understand, ask your teacher for clarity.
6. If you have a separate answer sheet, check the number of the question on the test with the number on your answer sheet each time you mark an answer. Ask if you could use a slider or paper ruler to pinpoint or isolate

the number on the answer sheet. After you do the first five questions, go back and check to be sure that your numbers and answers are correct.
7. Answer the easiest questions first.
8. Every 10 minutes, stop and reflect.
9. Stay focused and alert. Do not be afraid to stop, breathe out, and stretch. Know your learning style (i.e., active or reflective) or multiple intelligence (i.e., kinesthetic). If you need a short break, stop for a minute and regroup. If you are a reflective learner, be aware of time so you don't get bogged down on any one question. If you are an active learner, be aware of careless mistakes due to rushing. Such individuals often become competitive and try to finish the test first, as it is their style. Learn from your mistakes!
10. Read each question carefully, and be sure you understand it. If you still do not understand a question, then put the question in your own words. Example: "The Emancipation Proclamation is a document that was signed by President Lincoln to abolish all slavery in the USA. What would our country be like today if this document was never enacted?"
11. Answer the question that was asked. Write only what is important to the answer. Be careful about giving too much of an opinion. Teachers want to see the most concrete response. Also, you are on the clock. Some teachers like to hear students' opinions. Therefore, do your homework about teacher expectations.
12. Split questions into parts. A math word problem may require several steps. Decide the steps that are needed and then concentrate on them one step at a time.
13. If you cannot answer a question, ask yourself the question in a different way. Look for clues in the question itself, or look for clues in the previous test material.
14. You may guess if grading is based on only right answers. Don't guess if wrong answers are subtracted from right answers.
15. On an essay or problem test, write what you can, even if you cannot write the entire answer. You could get a grade for effort.
16. Partial answers are better than blank answers; however, do not write nonsense. Check to see that you answered all questions and filled in all the blanks.

Strategy #7: Math Tests

Here is checklist of skills and strategies for solving math tests.

1. Read each question carefully. Decide what you have to solve. Decide what you have to do, how many steps you will need, and in what order they should be. Remember that you are dealing with concrete numbers and steps.
2. Ignore any information you do not need and place the pieces of information you do need in the proper order.
3. Use sketches to help you, especially with word problems.
4. If you get stuck, go back to the beginning of the problem and try working the problem out in a different way.
5. Check your math. Be neat. Draw a circle or a box around the answer so that it is not confused with other answers.
6. Be sure you answer the question that was asked. If the question is, "How many gallons of milk will you need to buy to serve 18 people?" the answer should be in gallons and not in quarts.
7. Don't spend too much time on any one problem.

Strategy #8

Do neat work. A number out of alignment may change your correct understanding of a problem into an incorrect answer.

Strategy #9

Be sure to put the correct units with the numerical answer, such as four inches or five gallons.

Strategy #10: Research Study Techniques

Research conducted by John Dunlosky and associates at Kent State University described how certain study techniques could accelerate learning that could be supportive of retention with test-taking while others simply do not. One study asked students to memorize word pairs—half of which were included on a recall test. One week later, students remembered 35 percent of the words they had quizzed themselves on at home but remembered only 4 percent of those words that they had not included in their self-quizzing.

Why does self-quizzing work? Practice at testing oneself triggers mental search of long-term memory that activates related information, forming multiple memory pathways for easier access (Dunlosky and Rawson, 2005). The bottom line: All students can benefit from the practice of testing; the benefits may last for months to years. If nothing else, self-testing can give a student experience for the real tests to follow.

Another highly rated study technique is called "distributed practice." Students usually mass their studies or cram. Instead, with distributed practice, students who practice over time were more effective in the tests that followed. Researchers had students learn the English equivalent of Spanish words and then reviewed the material in six sessions. One group did the review sessions back-to-back, another one day apart, and a third did the reviews 30 days after. Students in the 30-day part remembered the translations the best. Of 254 studies involving more than 14,000 subjects, students remembered more after spaced study, scoring 47 percent versus 37 percent of students who massed their study.

The third highest rated technique is "elaborative interrogation." These two big words—"elaborative" and "interrogation"—suggest that students should use "why" questions (discussed earlier in this chapter) to facilitate learning. Why questions produce explanations for facts. "Why is it true?" In one factual test, students who used elaborative interrogation answered about 72 percent of questions correctly, compared to about 37 percent for other questions that had not used elaborative interrogation. Also, why questions get students to think outside of the box, which is good for tapping in to the higher centers of the brain.

"Self-explanation" was ranked fourth among best techniques. Students can develop explanations for what they learn with such questions as "What new information is provided here for greater learning?" and "How does it relate to what I already know?" Self-explanation is said to be beneficial for solving math problems, logical reasoning, and for learning from narratives. In younger children, self-explanation can help with basic ideas such as learning numbers or for recognizing patterns. In addition, self-explanation is said to improve memory, comprehension, and problem solving.

Brain Gains #126

Please Google *Dr. David Sortino: When Choosing the Wrong Answers Can Be Right!*

10

Left/Right-Brain Teaching

Take a moment to think about the entire school learning process that takes place from kindergarten through grade 12. The consensus is that most schools' curriculums are left hemisphere dominant, especially in the elementary school grades. (Our left hemisphere is responsible for analytical and sequential thinking and supports linguistic intelligence; whereas the right hemisphere is responsible for holistic and abstract thinking and supports our visual intelligence.)

Schools are structured environments that accommodate time schedules, favor facts over theories and rules over patterns, offering predominantly verbal instruction, especially at the secondary level. The end result is that left-hemisphere preferred learners (mainly girls) feel more comfortable in this environment. The stronger the left hemisphere, the more successful these learners can be. Conversely, right hemisphere learners (mainly boys) are not comfortable in such environments. Bottom line: The stronger the left hemisphere preference in a learning environment, the less successful the learning experience appears.

—*David Sousa, 2015*

This last chapter makes the case to support Dr. David Sousa's opening quote to this chapter as to why educators need to break out of a "one-dimensional," left-side teaching philosophy and employ a "multisensory approach" by addressing both sides of a student's brain. Studies show that when you address both sides of the brain, you not only create better learners, you also improve their success in other aspects of their lives due to increased self-esteem, organization, long-range planning, positive peer relationships, improved social skills, and so on.

However, with mandated curriculums, shortened school years, mandated testing, addressing both sides of a student's brain, or taking a multisensory teaching approach is often in direct conflict with present school curriculums.

Most school curriculums and teaching lessons are connected to the school year (180 days), length of day (six hours), and mandated testing (one time yearly for about two weeks to measure school performance). However, the problem for most teachers is time and knowledge as to how to integrate teaching lessons to support both sides of their students' brains. To sum up, the majority of teaching often revolves around these three factors (mandated curriculums, shortened school years, mandated testing), which again is in direct conflict when addressing both sides of your students' brains.

Again, in my opinion, the most effective approach to reaching both sides of your students' brains is to employ multisensory teaching approaches that include an attempt to incorporate multisensory approaches, such as the visual, auditory, and kinesthetic to school lessons.

Brain Gains #127

Experts believe that students remember what they learn while using multiple senses more effectively than while using one sense. There is scientific evidence that multisensory teaching is the perfect brain food for learning. According to research, neuroimaging studies have shown that there is a greater amount of activity in the brains information processing areas following a multisensory input than there is following a single-sense input (Willis, 2007).

Briefly, teaching others was the most successful teaching approach that enlisted both sides of the students' brains; ironically, the lecture format (5 percent) is currently the most popular teaching approach in the majority of our schools. (Note: See entry 1 in the Appendix for a detailed version of the Pyramid of Learning.)

My last example is a personal left/right-brain teaching experience, when I employed a driver's education lesson with learning handicap (LH) and severely emotionally disturbed (SED) students at a state regional school for exceptional children. (Note to reader: This personal experience is taken from my book called *The Promised Cookie: No Longer Angry Children*, 2011.) My publication describes several teaching experiences that support left- and right-brain teaching.

It was only my second week as a first-year teacher at a day treatment program for seriously emotionally disturbed and learning handicapped students, ages 14 to 19. I was hired to teach math, English, and science to a class of 14 students. I had tried to teach from the school's textbooks; however, the students voiced their displeasure vociferously about "how teachers had previously tried to teach from the textbooks and they had learned nothing!" They demanded that I teach them "something they could use in real life!" In fact, they were so adamant about their proposal, some actually threw their books on the floor or out of the classroom windows!

I found a driver's education manual, and the next day, instead of teaching math, English, and science, I began reading questions from a driver's education manual. Within seconds, the students began shouting out the answers to the questions. This response continued for the entire 55-minute period. In fact, they didn't want to go on break but instead demanded I ask them more questions because "we need to get our driver's licenses and drive to California!"

However, I needed to support the math, English, science, and history classes! Therefore, I brought in a 30-foot by 3-foot roll of butcher paper and let them draw and plot car routes and distances to California. For English class, they were required to write about important city sites along the car routes. For math, they had to compute cost of gas, tolls, hotel bills, food, and so on for their drive to California. For science, they studied and wrote about the difference in climates, ecosystems, and animal life on their journey. And for history, they were required to write about historical facts associated with the major cities en route to California.

The entire lesson took about six weeks. At the conclusion of the class, we had a parents' night, and the students proudly lectured about what they learned on their car trip to California!

From the students' perspective, "it was the best school experienced we ever had because you taught us something we could use in life!"

I used Key's 1991 left/right-brain teaching techniques (discussed in the following section) to support my successful driver's education lesson.

1. Practice Efficient Classroom Organization

The driver's education lesson immediately created a sense of order and organization due to my students' increased interest in the lesson, which was reflected in their demand for organization and desire to complete the driver's education lesson.

Related Research: Here are five steps to organize and to open your mind, and keep yourself on track for a productive day.

1. Find the right amount of challenge in what you do
2. Take control of your emotions
3. Sustain focus
4. Take breaks
5. Shift sets

2. Use Relevant Bulletin Boards

The driver's education lesson used 3-foot by 30-foot butcher paper to display all of the students' schoolwork. In addition, the students drew car routes (visual—right brain) as well as documented historical information (linguistic—left brain). The lesson even satisfied the students' kinesthetic intelligence because they had to be out of their desks for long periods of time drawing, writing their papers on the large classroom floor, and so on.

Related Research: People with visual/spatial intelligence are very aware of their surroundings and are good at remembering images. They have a keen sense of direction and often enjoy maps. They have a sharp sense of space, distance, and measurement. People with visual intelligence learn well through visual aids such as graphs, diagrams, pictures, and maps/colorful displays. They usually enjoy visual arts such as drawing, painting, and photography. They can visualize anything related to art, fashion, decoration, and culinary design before creating it (Personality Max, n.d.).

3. Use Multisensory Approaches

The driver's education class represented a multisensory approach to support all of the students' intelligences. Again, they drew car routes (i.e., kinesthetic, artistic, spatial, lingustic, mathematical) from Connecticut to California, adding geographic and historical sites of the cities and towns they traveled through, as well as computing mileage, hotel bills, tolls, food, etc. Furthermore, they worked with a partner to support the intra- and interpersonal intelligences.

LEFT/RIGHT-BRAIN TEACHING 115

Related Research: "Multisensory teaching isn't just limited to reading and listening. Instead, it tries to use all of the senses. Every lesson will not be able to use movement. But in most multisensory lessons, students engage with the material in more than one way. For example, let's say your child's class is studying apples. Your child might have the chance to visually examine, touch, smell and taste apples—instead of just reading and listening to his teacher speak about how they grow. Then he might hold a halved apple and count the number of seeds inside, one by one" (Morin, 2019).

4. Support Interpersonal Skills

The driver's education lesson supported interpersonal skills because the students worked in teams and communicated with their partners about their project.

Related Research: Interpersonal intelligence is defined as a type of intelligence when certain individuals are skillful in understanding others, such as psychologists, writers, philosophers, and poets, which are among those of Dr. Howard Gardner's nine intelligences as having high interpersonal intelligence (Thought Company, 2019).

5. Use Metaphors and Analogies

The driver's education lesson was a metaphorical experience for my teens because obtaining a driver's license would allow them to drive cross country from Connecticut to California. In many ways, the potential to obtain a driver's license could be a metaphor for adulthood.

Related Research: "Recognizing and constructing analogies is one way of helping students bridge between the new and the old. Traditional analogies include the eye and a camera, the heart and a pump, the brain and a computer, and memory and a file cabinet. Self-created analogies are generally more effective than those made up by others" (Gunning, 1996).

6. Emphasize Punctuality

The driver's education lesson facilitated student enthusiasm for school and class attendance because the students demanded that we stay on a strict schedule to complete their project for an upcoming teacher/parent school night.

Related Research: "Missing a day of school here and there or arriving 10 minutes late may seem inconsequential and at times even insignificant, but consider this: a student who is 10 minutes late every day will miss over 30 hours of instruction during the year—a week of school. A student who is absent just twice a month will miss 20 school days—4 weeks of school! Each lateness or absence means a student has lost an opportunity to learn. Just as we can never regain a moment of time wasted, missing a day of school means missing a day of education that cannot be retrieved. Students may be able to make up an assignment, but they can never recover what is most important—the discussion, the questions, the explanations by the teacher and the thinking that makes learning come alive" (Totten Public Schools, 2018).

7. Encourage Goal-Setting

The driver's education lesson motivated the students to complete the goal of finishing their projects on time for our monthly parent/teacher night.

Related Research: "Educators all have high hopes for their students and want to help them grow toward their dreams. Goal-setting is an important part of short- and long-term achievement for students in life and academics. However, teacher training and professional development has not traditionally provided guidance on how to help students set goals or monitor their progress" (Christo, 2019).

8. Promote Logical Thinking

The driver's education lesson provided the students with the opportunity to apply logical thinking, such as researching car routes that included speed limits and traffic patterns as well as when and where to stay in hotels.

Related Research: "As teachers plan, they look at the standards for the content they teach and think about the large overarching topics that are foundational to their specific grade/subject. For each of those foundational topics, teachers should have a few anchor tasks, activities, and/or investigations that provide meaningful experiences for their students" (Jones, 2017).

2. KEY'S RIGHT-BRAIN TEACHING TECHNIQUES TO SUPPORT THE DRIVER EDUCATION LESSON.

1. Give Students Some Options

The driver's education lesson gave the students options to drive to San Francisco or Los Angeles as well as choices as to where to stop and visit cities on their journey.

Related Research: "One study revealed that giving simple choices to students in math computer tasks normalized the behaviors of students diagnosed with ADHD. Another study reported that when students were allowed to choose their art material, they produced more creative art projects. Give students opportunities to choose their own books to read, and create experiments to conduct; allow them to create vocabulary lists and math problems to solve" (Armstrong, 2018).

2. Use Visual Variety

The students placed their car routes and historical sites onto butcher paper (i.e., visual representation). Also, they experienced what their trip to California could look like as their 3,000-plus miles were reduced in size to accommodate the length of the 30-foot by 30-foot strips of paper. Also, the opportunity to draw important historical sites in cities and towns stimulated the visual intelligence.

Related Research: "Our brains are wired to rapidly make sense of and remember visual input. Visualizations in the form of diagrams, charts, drawings, pictures, and a variety of other mediums can help students understand complex information. A well-designed visual image can yield a much more powerful and memorable learning experience than a mere verbal or textual description" (Ebner and Bruff, 2019).

3. Encourage Direct Experiences

The driver's education lesson could not have been more direct since all the students wanted to obtain their driver's licenses and drive cross country to California.

Related Research: "Experiential education, as defined by the Association for Experiential Education (AEE), encompasses the educator as well as the learner and is 'a philosophy that informs many methodologies in which educators purposefully engage with learners in direct experience and focused reflection in order to increase knowledge, develop skills, clarify values, and develop people's capacity to contribute to their communities'" (Rutland and Gross, 2017).

4. Allow Student Teaching

Older students were paired with younger students to allow for our older students to teach and share information with the younger ones.

Related Research: "Students teaching students easily applied to all types of learners. I would recommend a few things to keep in mind as other teachers' experiment with this process.

"One: Help students understand the difference between presenting and learning how to teach a lesson.

"Two: Provide enough time for students to learn the topic they have been assigned to completely educate themselves and their peers.

"Three: Provide adequate resources for the students to peruse as they are putting their lessons together.

"Four: I would recommend that as students are listening to the lessons, they make notes on the material presented so they can thoughtfully reflect and ask questions. Lastly, try to ensure that your students are challenged by their lesson and can really learn from their own information. 'To foster intellectual development, youth need to interact directly with their world through discourse and hands-on experience with their peers'" (Stevenson, 2002).

5. Allow Ease in Timing

The driver's education lesson was scheduled every day for two hours with a 30-minute break. I did not want to lose the passion and interest by shortening or lengthening the lesson's time. In addition, I scheduled the lesson to last four weeks to coincide with our monthly parent/teacher conference.

Related Research: "Time is a precious commodity for teachers. Most teachers would argue that they never have enough time to reach every student, particularly the ones that are below grade level. Therefore, every second a teacher has with their students should be a meaningful and productive second" (Meador, 2019).

6. Incorporate Hands-On Learning

The driver's education lesson was geared to support "hands-on learning" since the students were constructing the lesson on butcher paper.

Related Research: "Hands-on learning has proven that students who are taught using hands-on teaching methods with manipulatives outperform those who do not use manipulatives. It is also true for many subjects but most documented in mathematics" (Claessens, Engel, and Curran, 2013).

7. Encourage Direct Experiences

The driver's education lesson helped the students to participate in what I liked to call "experiential learning," or "learning by doing."

Related Research: "In its simplest form, experiential learning means learning from experience or learning by doing. Experiential education first immerses learners in an experience and then encourages reflection about the experience to develop new skills, new attitudes, or new ways of thinking" (Lewis and Williams, 1994).

8. Allow for Imaginative Solutions

The driver's education lesson could not have been more imaginative for teens who wanted to obtain their driver's licenses as well as drive to California.

Related Research: "Education to foster creativity can range from simple team-building exercises to complex, open-ended problems that may require a semester to solve. An instructor that presents innovative and challenging prompts will encourage students to work creatively through a problem to a solution. These creative techniques must be done in a supportive environment with appropriate time allocated for students to discover and develop creative ways to solve a problem" that allows for imaginative solutions ("14 Creative Ways to Engage Students," 2019).

Brain Gains #128

Boys outnumber girls ten to one in remedial and special education programs.

Brain Gains #129

What do we need in order to learn? Attention! Our attention must be activated in order to learn. MSL demands attention and focus in a way that is engaging and enjoyable. It stimulates the RAD system (Reticular Activating System) in our brain. This is the fight or flight part of the brain. We are wired to survive without reading. Therefore, we need to create a teaching/learning climate that is low-stress, fun, and novel. Multisensory learning is a perfect recipe for feeding our RAD system. If a student is engaging in a physical or tactile activity, as well as listening, seeing images, and speaking, there is not much of an opportunity for their attention to wander (Willis, 2007).

1. Cognitive Benefits When You Address Both Sides of Your Students' Brains
2. Psycho-Social Benefits When You Address Left and Right Brain Teaching
3. Gardner's Multiple Intelligence Theory Supports L/R Brain Teaching
4. How Dr. Robert Feldman's Eight Learning Styles Support L/R-Brain Teaching
5. An Example of a Left/Right-Brain Public School Science Lesson

3. LEFT/RIGHT-BRAIN ASSESSMENT

The conclusion to this chapter is for readers to now have the opportunity to test themselves on their particular mode of learning with what they have learned about left- and right-brain teaching.

From each pair below, circle a or b corresponding to the sentence that best describes you. Answer all questions. There are no right or wrong answers.

1. A. I prefer to find my own way of doing a new task.
   B. I prefer to be told the best way to do a new task.
2. A. I have to make my own plans.
   B. I can follow anyone's plans.
3. A. I am very a flexible and occasionally unpredictable person.
   B. I am a very stable and consistent person.
4. A. I keep everything in a particular place.
   B. Where I keep things depends on what I am doing.
5. A. I spread my work evenly over the time I have.
   B. I prefer to do my work at the last minute.
6. A. I know I am right because I have good reasons.
   B. I know when I am right, even without reasons.
7. A. I need a lot of variety and change in my life.
   B. I need a well-planned and orderly life.
8. A. I sometimes have too many ideas in a new situation.
   B. I sometimes don't have any ideas in a new situation.
9. A. I do easy things first and important things last.
   B. I do the important things first and the easy things last.
10. A. I choose what I know is right when making a hard decision.
    B. I choose what I feel is right when making a hard decision.
11. A. I plan my time for doing my work.
    B. I don't think about the time when I work.

12. A. I usually have good self-discipline.
    B. I usually act on my feelings.
13. A. Other people don't understand how I organize things.
    B. Other people think I organize things well.
14. A. I agree with new ideas before other people do.
    B. I question new ideas more than other people do.
15. A. I tend to think more in pictures.
    B. I tend to think more in words.
16. A. I try to find the one best way to solve a problem.
    B. I try to find different ways to solve a problem.
17. A. I can usually analyze what is going to happen next.
    B. I can usually sense what is going to happen next.
18. A. I am not very imaginative in my work.
    B. I use my imagination in nearly everything I do.
19. A. I begin many jobs that I never finish.
    B. I finish a job before starting a new one.
20. A. I look for new ways to do old jobs.
    B. When one way works well, I don't change it.
21. A. It is fun to take risks.
    B. I have fun without taking risks.

Left/Right-Brain Scoring

Count the number of A responses to questions 1, 3, 7, 8, 9, 13, 14, 15, 19, 20, and 21. Place that number on the line to the right. Count the number of B responses to the remaining questions. Place the number on the line to the right. Total the A and B questions you counted. The total indicates your hemispheric preference according to the following scale.

0 – 5:   Strong left hemisphere preference

6 – 8:   Moderate left hemisphere preference

9 – 12: Bilateral hemisphere balance (little or no preference)

13 – 15: Moderate right hemisphere preference

16 – 21: Strong right hemispheric preference

TOTAL: _____

Appendix

#1: THE PYRAMID OF LEARNING

    Verbal Processing = Lecture = 5%

    Verbal Processing = Reading = 10%

    Verbal and Visual Processing = Demonstration = 30%

    Verbal and Visual Processing = Discussion Group = 50%

    Doing = Practice by Doing = 75%

    Doing = Teach/Others/Immediate Use of Learning = 90%

The average retention rate after 24 hours shows that students will only remember 5 percent of a lecture. Interestingly, verbal processing is the major approach in most high school classes. The second level, also associated with verbal processing, is reading with a 10 percent retention rate. The third level combines verbal and visual processing or the audio-visual and has a 30 percent retention rate.

#2: COGNITIVE BENEFITS WHEN YOU ADDRESS BOTH SIDES OF YOUR STUDENTS' BRAINS

When you address both sides, you also increase the students' cognitive development. For example, in this lesson, the teacher applied a multisensory approach (i.e., kinesthetic, auditory, etc.) when addressing both sides of the students' brains. Support for this is seen in this example called "The Bat Lesson." The findings of this approach amplify the importance of a left/right-brain teaching content to stimulate the students' cognitive and/or thinking development.

At the beginning of a lesson about species, a fifth-grade science teacher asked the class to make up criteria for classification of the following animals:

Bat

Cow

Robin

Hawk

Dog

The majority of the students said "walking and flying" or "two legs or four legs." The students viewed the world logically and concretely, or *two perspectives* at one time. However, a small percentage of this class saw other criteria. They knew that a bat can fly; yet, it is also a mammal.

This group had the ability to see abstract criteria (i.e., right side) in classifying the groups by species. The ability to classify the group into species is a major step up from concrete thinking. Instead of entertaining two ideas at one time, they could entertain three ideas or could use formal operations. The teacher discovered that *even* after she had taught the 10- to 11-year-old age group about species, three to four weeks later, 90 percent of the students who were thinking at concrete operations forgot and still classified the animals as "walking or flying."

The teacher decided to bring in a live bat or present a multisensory teaching (i.e., left/right-brain teaching strategy). Adding a live bat to the equation integrated other intelligences (e.g., kinesthetic, visual, smell, etc.) to the lesson and helped stimulate the children's understanding that bats must be categorized as a species and, as such, are mammals. They have hair and give birth to their young (instead of laying eggs) as well as nurse their young.

Further, they do not have scales or feathers, are warm-blooded, and can regulate their own body temperature. Five weeks later, the teacher asked the same class to classify the same animals, and 100 percent of the students classified the animals according to species.

#3: AN EXAMPLE OF A LEFT/RIGHT-BRAIN PUBLIC SCHOOL SCIENCE LESSON

An excellent teaching example to support left- and right-brain curriculum development is described by a lesson on the solar system.

Let's say, for example, that you are introducing a unit on the solar system. Here are some left-brain and right-brain teaching techniques that will help strong to moderate left-brain/right-brain students feel engaged during your lesson.

Left-Brain Teaching Approaches

Write an outline of the lesson on the board. Students with left-brain strengths appreciate sequence.

- Go ahead and lecture! These students love to listen to an expert and take notes.
- Discuss vocabulary words and create a crossword puzzle on the solar system.
- Assign individual assignments so students may work alone.
- Ask the students to write a research paper on the solar system that includes both detail and conceptual analysis.
- Keep the room relatively quiet and orderly. Many students with left-brain strengths prefer not to hear other conversations when working on a stimulating project.

Right-Brain Teaching Approaches

Taking the solar system example, here are some right-brain teaching techniques that will help students with moderate to strong right-brain strengths get the most out of your lesson:

- During the lecture, either write the main points on the board or pass out a study guide outline that students can fill in as you present orally. These visual clues will help students focus even though you are lecturing.
- Use the overhead, the whiteboard, or the chalkboard frequently. Since the students are apt to miss the points discussed verbally, the visual pointers will help the students "see" and comprehend the points.

- Discuss the big concepts involved in the creation of the universe, how the solar system was formed, and so on. Right-brain students love to think about and discuss abstract concepts. Have some time for group activities during the week of the solar system study. Right-brain students enjoy the company of others.
- Let the students create a project (such as a poster, a mobile, a diorama, or papier-mâché planets of the solar system) in lieu of writing a paper. Right-brained students often have excellent hand-eye coordination.
- Play music, such as the theme from *2001: A Space Odyssey*. Discuss how space might feel to an astronaut. Students with right-brain strengths are intuitive and like to get in touch with their feelings during the day.
- Bring in charts and maps of the universe and let the students find the Milky Way. Maps and graphs make use of the students' strong right-brain visual-spatial skills.

#4: PUBLIC SCHOOL ATTENDANCE POLICY

At West Sonoma County Public Schools and Analy High School Sebastopol in California, students are required to attend classes in accordance with compulsory full-time education laws (Ed. Code 48200). Categories for attendance accountability include the following:

1. Excused: An excused absence is defined under Board Policy. The teacher is to allow a student to make up the work missed during absences to the degree possible for such work to be completed. An excused absence shall be granted for the following reasons:
   A. Personal illness
   B. Quarantine under city or county direction
   C. Medical, dental, or optometry services
   D. Exclusion for not having been properly immunized
   E. Attending funeral service of an immediate family member
   F. Required court appearance
   H. For a student who is the custodial parent of a child who is ill or has a medical appointment during school hours

APPENDIX

2. Warranted: A warranted absence, requested in writing prior to the absence, requires approval in advance by a school administrator. These include, but are not limited to the following:
   A. Employment conference or interview
   B. Religious holiday or celebration
   C. College visits (limited to three days per year)
   D. Bereavement beyond excused absence days
   E. Any absence under this section that is not requested in advance and in writing will be considered unexcused, and work may be made up only at the teacher's discretion.

3. Unexcused: Unexcused absences include, but are not limited to the following:
   A. Oversleeping
   B. Cutting
   C. Lack of transportation, care of siblings, other non-illness absences
   D. Family trips and vacations
   E. Any absence that is not cleared within five days after the student returns to school

4. Suspensions: According to Board Policy, the teacher of any class from which a student is suspended may require the suspended student to complete any assignments and tests missed during the suspension (Ed Code 48913). Suspensions are treated as warranted absences.

Excusing a Student Absence

It is the obligation of the parent or guardian of an absent student to excuse a student's absence with a written note or phone call to the attendance office, no later than 5 school days following the student's return to school. The note must be brought to the Attendance Office, should be easily read, and should include the student's first and last name, date(s) absent, and the reason(s) for the absence(s). Written notes may be brought to the Attendance Office at any time during the school day when class is not in session. No student may be excused from class by a parent and still remain on campus.

Short-Term Independent Studies

Independent study for anticipated absence is appropriate only when a student will be absent from school for five or more consecutive days with a maximum of 20 school days in a school year. A Master Agreement for Independent Study Contract must be submitted at least five days in advance of the absence. (See Board Policy 6158.)

Permit to Leave/Appointments

To take a student from school during the day, the parent/guardian must send a note with the student stating the time the student should be released and the reason. A telephone call or a personal contact by a parent will also be acceptable. The student needs to sign out at the attendance office before leaving and sign in upon return to school. A cut is issued if a student leaves campus without signing out at the Attendance Office and will be subjected to unexcused absence consequences.

Truancy—Definition

Truancy is defined as three or more days of unexcused absences. Truant students and their parents may have to appear before a School Attendance Review Board and may be reported to the district attorney. Unexcused absences or cuts may result in loss of academic credit and loss of a student's work permit.

Closed Campus

Students are not allowed to leave campus during the school day unless they obtain a "Permit to Leave" from the attendance office or health office or have an "Off Campus Permit" for unscheduled classes. Failure to follow check-out procedure could result in disciplinary action.

#5: A FORMAL STUDY TO COMPARE STUDENTS' DOMINANCE PROFILES TO SUPPORT LEFT- AND RIGHT-BRAIN CLASS PLACEMENT

"The importance of addressing both sides of a student's brain is revealed by a study conducted by Dr. Carla Hannaford, who, in 1994, conducted a formal study to compare students' dominance profiles with terms used by schools to classify and sort their learners. She wanted to discover the impact of brain dominance awareness in the success rate with such groups as Gifted and Talented or Special Education students.

"For those of us who like the bottom line in the beginning, what Carla Hannaford discovered was that overall, people with logic hemisphere dominant [left-brain dominant] profiles were heavily represented in the Gifted and Talented category, whereas students with right-brained or sensory-limited profiles were heavily represented in the Special Education groups.

"In the test, gifted and talented kids were 78 percent left-brained learners, while only 22 percent were right-brained learners. 'Normal' learners (i.e., kids doing fine in regular classrooms) were split 60/30 between left-brained and right-brained learners. "Remedial" (i.e., kids in Title 1 and kids with specific reading difficulties) were split about 56/44 between left- and right-brained learners. Special Education was a mirror image of Gifted and Talented learners, with only 22 percent left-brained learners and the remainder right-brained learners" (Child 1st, 2016).

#6: PSYCHOSOCIAL BENEFITS WHEN YOU ADDRESS LEFT- AND RIGHT-BRAIN TEACHING

Another theory that would support L/R-brain teaching is Erik Erikson's psychosocial theory. Erikson's developmental theory identified eight stages of psychological development. His stage called "Industry versus Inferiority" is particularly pertinent to this chapter on left/right-brain teaching because of the two particular age groups of my students who participated in the driver's education lesson. Erikson describes the two stages:

Stage 4: Early School Years: Industry vs. Inferiority

As children grow in independence, they become increasingly aware of themselves as individuals. They begin to compare themselves with others.

- **Industry**: Children who are accomplished compared to their peers can develop self-confidence and pride. Praise for their achievements can boost their self-esteem.
- **Inferiority**: Children who do not achieve certain milestones may doubt their abilities or self-worth. When children are constantly criticized, they may develop feelings of inferiority.

Stage 5: Adolescence: Identity vs. Role Confusion

The famed term "identity crisis" comes from this period of development. During this stage, adolescents' main goal is to answer the question "Who am I?" They may try different personas to determine which roles fit them best.

- **Identity:** To succeed in this stage, adolescents need to establish a coherent sense of self. They will need to determine their priorities in life (i.e., family, academic success, etc.). Then they will need to set goals for their adult selves based on those values.
- **Role confusion:** Some adolescents may have a weak sense of self. They may struggle to break away from the person their parents or peers expect them to be. Without a consistent identity, they may grow confused about what they truly want for the future.

#7: GARDNER'S MULTIPLE INTELLIGENCE THEORY SUPPORTS L/R-BRAIN TEACHING

It would be helpful for teachers and parents to familiarize themselves with Dr. Howard Gardner's Multiple Intelligence Theory as a strategy to incorporate his theory to support left/right-brain teaching content. Dr. Gardner proposes eight different intelligences to account for a broader range of human potential in children and adults.

Gardner's eight multiple intelligence are as follows:

- Linguistic intelligence ("word smart")
- Logical-mathematical intelligence ("number/reasoning smart")
- Spatial intelligence ("picture smart")
- Bodily-kinesthetic intelligence ("body smart")
- Musical intelligence ("music smart")
- Interpersonal intelligence ("people smart")
- Intrapersonal intelligence ("self smart")
- Naturalist intelligence ("nature smart")

* Thomas Armstrong, Ph.D., 2018

* For additional information concerning Multiple Intelligence, readers can consult the following: MIDAS website: http://www.youtube.com/watch?v=MSNVeaiJ-pU.

* Listen: Interview on WKSU: "Room for multiple intelligence in governor's reform plan": http://www.wksu.org/news/story/22959
* Check out: www.facebook.com/themidasprofile/

#8: HOW DR. ROBERT FELDMAN'S EIGHT LEARNING STYLES SUPPORT L/R-BRAIN TEACHING

Dr. Feldman addresses both sides of students' brains to support a richer and more realistic content in teaching and curriculum development. For additional information about learning styles, readers can return to chapter eight of this book. Below are Feldman's eight learning styles:

1. Active Learning Style: Improves retention and understanding of information by discussing or explaining it to others.
2. Reflective Learning Style: Prefers to think about the material first.
3. Sensory Learning Style: Benefits from learning facts and solving problems using well-established methods; enjoy courses that have connections to the real world.
4. Intuitive Learning Style: Prefers discovering possibilities and relationships; like innovation and abstract information.
5. Visual Learning Style: Likes to learn through pictures, diagrams, flow charts etc.
6. Verbal Learning Style: Prefers learning facts and solving problems using well-established methods.
7. Sequential Learning Style: Gains understanding in linear, logical steps, etc.
8. Global Learning Style: Learns in large jumps, randomly absorbing material until he/she suddenly *gets it*.

For further information, readers can Google *Dr. Richard Felder's free Learning Styles Assessment*.

#9: THE FOLLOWING SCHOOL PROGRAMS SUPPORT L/R-BRAIN LEARNING

Waldorf Education

One school that supports left/right-brain teaching approaches is Waldorf or Rudolf Steiner education, which is based on an anthroposophical view, or an understanding of the human being as a being of body, soul and spirit. The education mirrors the basic stages of a child's development from childhood to adulthood, which in general, reflects the development of humanity through history from our origin, far back in the past and up to the present.

The central focus for the Waldorf teacher is the development of that essence in every person that is independent of external appearance. Waldorf teachers instill in his/her pupils an understanding of and appreciation for their background and place in the world, not primarily as members of any specific nation, ethnic group, or race, but as members of humanity and world citizens.

Montessori

The Montessori method of education is named after Dr. Maria Montessori (1895–1934). She was the first woman in Italy to obtain the degree of doctor of medicine. Because she was a doctor, Dr. Montessori looked at education from a scientific level. She believed that education should prepare a person for all aspects of life. She designed materials and techniques that would promote a natural growth of learning in students. These materials are common to all Montessori classrooms. Working with these materials and techniques forms a pattern that children carry over naturally to reading, writing, and mathematics. Each skill is developed to interlock with another.

International Baccalaureate, or IB

The IB program was created in Switzerland in 1968 for students in international schools. The IB program is now offered in 3,460 schools across 143 countries—with 1,370 public and private schools (and counting) in the United States. IB has gained popularity for setting high standards and emphasizing creative and critical thinking. IB students are responsible for their own learning, choosing topics and devising their own projects, while teachers act more as supervisors or mentors than sources of facts. IB emphasizes research and encourages students to learn from their peers, with students actively critiquing one another's work. Beyond preparing students for critical thinking and college-level work, the full IB program calls for students to express themselves through writing, requires community service, and aims "to develop inquiring, knowledgeable and caring young people who help to create a better and more peaceful world through intercultural understanding and respect."

Bibliography

"14 Creative Ways to Engage Students." (2019). Iowa State University. https://www.celt.iastate.edu/teaching/teaching-format/14-creative-ways-to-engage-students/.

Alberta Education (2013). "Take Ten Series—Can Learn Society." Alberta, Canada.

Amen, D. (2018). "Amen Clinics." Walnut Creek, CA.

American Masters for Teachers. (n.d.). "The Importance of Using Multiple Methods of Reading Instruction." *PBS*. http://www.pbs.org/wnet/americanmasters/education/general.html.

American Pregnancy Association. (2019). "Breastfeeding: Overview." American Pregnancy Association. https://americanpregnancy.org/breastfeeding/breastfeeding-overview/.

Armstrong, T. (2018). "8 Ways to Boost Student Engagement by Giving Students Choices." American Institute for Learning and Human Development. May 4. https://www.institute4learning.com/2018/05/04/8-ways-to-boost-student-engagement-by-giving-students-choices/.

Arrington, D. (n.d.). "Thalamus: Definition, Functions & Location Video, Chapter 5, Lesson 8." Study.com. https://study.com/academy/lesson/thalamus-definition-functions-location.html.

Asaridou, S. A., and J. M. McQueen. (2013). "Speech and Music Shape the Listening Brain: Evidence for Shared Doman-General Mechanisms." *Frontiers of Psychology*, Vol. 4 (June 4): 321.

Atkinson, R. C., and R. M. Shiffrin. (1971). "The Central Processes of Short-Term Memory." Institute for Mathematical Studies in the Social Sciences. Stanford University. Palo Alto, CA.

Bailey, R. (2019). "Parietal Lobes of the Brain." ThoughtCo. May 8. https://www.thoughtco.com/parietal-lobes-of-the-brain-3865903.

Barnes, S. (2017). "Taurine & Breastfeeding." Healthfully.com. June 13. https://healthfully.com/476695-taurine-breastfeeding.html.

Brannon, E. J., and G. Van der Wale (2001). "Ordinal Numerical Knowledge in Young Children." *Cognitive Psychology*, Vol. 43: 53–81.

Brighton College (2018). "Study Tips for Verbal Learners." Scottsdale, AZ.

Brookshire, B. (2016). "Hormone Affects How Teens' Brains Control Emotions." Science News for Students. July 15. https://www.sciencenewsforstudents.org/article/hormone-affects-how-teens-brains-control-emotions.

Butterworth, B. (1999). *What Counts: How Every Brain Is Hardwired for Math.* New York: Free Press.

Carskadon, M. A. (2011). "Sleep in Adolescents: The Perfect Storm." *Pediatric Clinics of North America*, Vol. 58, No. 3 (June): 637–47.

Center for Disease Control and Prevention. (2015). *Sleep in Middle and High School Students.* https://www.cdc.gov/features/students-sleep/index.html.

Chaput, J. P., and C. Dutil. (2016). "Lack of sleep as a contributor to obesity in adolescents: impacts on eating and activity behaviors." *International Journal of Behavioral Nutrition and Physical Activity*, Vol. 13, No. 1 (September 26): 103.

Child 1st. (2016). "What Happens When We Teach a Right-Brained Learner in a Left-Brained Fashion?" February 4. https://child1st.com/blogs/resources/113578183-what-happens-when-we-teach-a-right-brained-learner-in-a-left-brained-fashion.

Christo, J. (2019). "Strategies to Support Student Goal Setting in the Classroom." *Teacher Vision.* January 25. https://www.teachervision.com/blog/morning-announcements/strategies-to-support-student-goal-setting.

Claessens, A., M. Engel, and F. C. Curran. (2013). "Academic Content, Student Learning, and the Persistence of Preschool Effects." *American Educational Research Journal*, Vol. 50, No. 6.

College Board. (2001). The College Board Profile of SAT and Achievement Test Takers for 2001.

Course Hero. (2019). Redwood City, CA.

Cowan, N. (2001). "The Magical Number Four in Short-term Memory: A Reconsideration of Mental Storage Capacity. *Behavioral and Brain Sciences*, 24. Available online at www.bbsonline.org/documents.

———. (2005). *Working Memory Capacity*. Hove, East Sussex, UK: Psychology Press.

Davis, N. (n.d.). "Is It Good to Listen to Music While Studying?" Study.com. https://study.com/academy/popular/is-it-good-to-listen-to-music-while-studying.html.

Dean, R. (2015). "5 Ways to Support Students with Sensory Processing Disorders." *TeachThought*. December 19. https://www.teachthought.com/pedagogy/5-ways-to-support-students-sensory-processing-disorder/.

Diamond, M. C., and J. Hopson. (1998). *Magic Trees of the Mind: How to Nurture Your Child's Intelligence, Creativity, and Healthy Emotions from Birth Through Adolescence*. New York: Plume.

Diproperzio, L. (n.d.). "The Benefits of Reading to Your Newborn." *Parents*. https://www.parents.com/baby/development/intellectual/benefits-of-reading-to-your-newborn/.

Dunlosky, J., and K. A. Rawson. (2005). "Why Does Rereading Improve Miscomprehension Accuracy? Evaluating the Levels-of-Disruption Hypothesis for the Rereading Effect." *Discourse Processes*, Vol. 40: 37–56.

Early Arts. (2017). "Creativity in Early Brain Development." March 30. https://earlyarts.co.uk/blog/creativity-in-early-brain-development.

Ebner, M., and D. Bruff. (2019). "Visual Thinking." https://cft.vanderbilt.edu/guides-sub-pages/visual-thinking/.

Education Corner. (2019). Saratoga Springs, Utah.

Edutopia. (2016). Marin County, CA.

Encyclopedia of Mental Disorders. (2019). "Phonological Disorder." http://www.minddisorders.com/Ob-Ps/Phonological-disorder.html.

Feinstein, S. (2009). *Inside the Teenage Brain: Parenting a Work in Progress*. Lanham, MD: Rowman & Littlefield.

Felder, R., and B. Solomon. (2008). *Learning Styles and Strategies*. Raleigh: North Carolina State University.

Fiske, R. D. (ed.). (1999). "Champions of Change: The impact of the Arts on Learning." Washington, DC: President's Committee on the Arts and the Humanities.

Fleming, G. (2019). "Analytic and Sequential Learning." *ThoughtCo*. January 31. https://www.thoughtco.com/analytic-and-sequential-learning-1857080.

Fulbright, R. K. et al. (1999). "The Cerebellum's Role in Reading: a Functional MR Imaging Study." *American Journal of Neuroradiology*, Vol. 20, No. 10 (November–December): 1925–30.

Gardner, H. (1983). *Frames of the Mind—The Theory of Multiple Intelligences*. New York: Basic Books.

Gaser, C., and G. Schlaug. (2003). "Brain Structures Differ between Musicians and Non-Musicians." *Journal of Neuroscience*, Vol. 23, No. 27 (October 8): 9240–9245.

Gazzaniga, M. (2008). *Learning, Arts, and the Brain*. New York: Dana Press.

Gersema, E. (2016). "Children's Brains Develop Faster with Music Training." USC News. June 20. https://news.usc.edu/102681/childrens-brains-develop-faster-with-music-training/.

Gholipour, B. (2016). "A Parent's Touch Actually Transforms a Baby's Brain." *Huffington Post*, July 29.

Glossary of Education Reform. (2015). "Hidden Curriculum." Last update July 13, 2015. https://www.edglossary.org/hidden-curriculum/.

Goldberg, E. (2001). *The Executive Brain: Frontal Lobes and the Civilized Mind*. New York: Oxford Press.

Goodman, B. (2011). "Study: ADHD Linked to Preterm Birth." *WebMD*. April 18. https://www.webmd.com/add-adhd/childhood-adhd/news/20110418/study-adhd-linked-preterm-birth.

Gunning, T. G. (1996). *Creating Reading Instruction for All Children*. Boston, MA: Allyn & Bacon.

Gupta, S. (2011). "Brain Region That Predicts the Future Identified." *New Scientist*. August 23. https://www.newscientist.com/article/dn20820-brain-region-that-predicts-the-future-identified/.

Gutow, J. (2017). University of Wisconsin. Madison: University of Wisconsin.

Harms, W. (2011). "Writing About Worries Eases Anxiety and Improves Test Performance." University of Chicago News. https://news.uchicago.edu/story/writing-about-worries-eases-anxiety-and-improves-test-performance/.

Harriman, P., and H. Ashbach. (2016). "Today's Parents Spend More Time with Their Kids Than Moms and Dads Did 50 Years Ago." *UCI News*. September 28. https://news.uci.edu/2016/09/28/todays-parents-spend-more-time-with-their-kids-than-moms-and-dads-did-50-years-ago/.

Hatfield, I. (2018). "The New American Cursive Writing Program." Louisville, KY.

Hawke, J. L. et al. (2009). "Gender Rations for Reading Difficulties." *Dyslexia*, Vol. 15, No. 3 (August): 239–42.

Heiting, G. (2019). *All About Vision*. Fullerton, CA: USC Press.

Hoecker, J. L. (2019). "I've Heard A Lot About the Terrible Twos. Why are 2-Year-Olds So Difficult?" *Mayo Clinic*. https://www.mayoclinic.org/healthy-lifestyle/infant-and-toddler-health/expert-answers/terrible-twos/faq-20058314.

International Dyslexia Association. (n.d.). "Definition of Dyslexia." https://dyslexiaida.org/definition-of-dyslexia/.

Jabr, F. (2011). "Cache Cab: Taxi Drivers' Brains Grow to Navigate London's Streets." *Scientific American*. December 8. https://www.scientificamerican.com/article/london-taxi-memory/.

Jantz, G. L. (2014). "Brain Differences Between Genders." *Psychology Today*. February 27. https://www.psychologytoday.com/us/blog/hope-relationships/201402/brain-differences-between-genders.

Jarrett, C. (2012). "Two Myths and Three Facts About the Differences in Men and Women's Brains." *Psychology Today*. July 20. https://www.psychologytoday.com/us/blog/brain-myths/201207/two-myths-and-three-facts-about-the-differences-in-men-and-womens-brains.

Jones, T. (2017). "Helping Students Develop Logical Reasoning." *Middleweb*. January 15. https://www.middleweb.com/33888/helping-students-develop-logical-reasoning/.

Kahn Academy. (n.d.). "Miller's Law, Chunking, and the Capacity of Working Memory." Kahn Academy. https://www.khanacademy.org/test-prep/mcat/social

-sciences-practice/social-science-practice-tut/e/miller-s-law--chunking--and-the-capacity-of-working-memory.

Kasanoff, B. (2017). "Intuition Is the Highest Form of Intelligence." *Forbes*. February 21, 2017.

Kent, J. (2017). "Perceptual Representation System." (In Quora). Mountain View, CA..

Klein, S. (2011). "Study: Too Many Video Games May Sap Attention Span." *Health*. http://www.cnn.com/2010/HEALTH/07/05/games.attention/.

Kohlberg, L. (1973). *Essays on Moral Development, I: The Philosophy of Moral Development: Moral Stages and the Idea of Justice*. San Francisco, CA: Harper & Row.

Lawson, C. (2002). "The Connections Between Emotions and Learning." Center for Development & Learning. January 1. https://www.cdl.org/articles/the-connections-between-emotions-and-learning/.

Learning Company. (2018). San Francisco, CA.

Learning Styles Online. (2019). "The Visual (Spatial) Learning Style." https://www.learning-styles-online.com/style/visual-spatial/.

Lewis, L. H., and C. J. Williams. (1994). "Experiential Learning: Past and Present." *New Directions for Adult & Continuing Education*, Vol. 1994, No. 62 (Summer): 5–16.

Lickona, T. (1983). *Raising Good Children: From Birth Through The Teenage Years*. New York: Bantam.

Lindamood, C., and P. Lindamood. (1975). *Auditory Discrimination in Depth. DSM Teaching Associates, Book 1—Understanding the Program*. New York: Teaching Resources Corp. Live Science.

Lohr, J. (2015). "Can Visualizing Your Body Doing Something Help You Learn to Do It Better?" *Scientific American Mind*. May 1. https://www.scientificamerican.com/article/can-visualizing-your-body-doing-something-help-you-learn-to-do-it-better/.

Macrae, F. (2012). "Bring Water into Exams to Improve your Grades." *Science Daily*. British Psychological Society.

Maguire, E. A., C. D. Frith, and R. G. Morris. (1999). "The Functional Neuroanatomy of Comprehension and Memory: The Importance of Prior Knowledge." *Brain*, Vol. 122, No. 10 (October 1): 1839–1850.

Martin, N. A., and R. Brownell. (2005). *(TAPS-3) Test of Auditory Processing Skills, Third Edition*. Torrance, CA: WPS Publishing.

Meador, D. (2019). "Strategies for Teachers to Maximize Student Learning Time." https://www.thoughtco.com/strategies-for-teachers-to-maximize-student-learning-time-4065667.

Michelon, P. (2006). "What Are Cognitive Abilities and Skills, and How to Boost Them." Sharp Brain. December 18. https://sharpbrains.com/blog/2006/12/18/what-are-cognitive-abilities/.

Miller, G. A. (1956). "The Magical Number Seven, Plus or Minus Two: Some Limits on Our Capacity for Processing Information." *Psychological Review*, Vol. 63, No. 2: 81–97.

Morin, A. (2019). *Underwood Multisensory Instruction: What You Need to Know*. New York, NY.

Morrison, M. (2015). "Primacy and Recency Effects in Learning." RapidBi.com. March 17. https://rapidbi.com/primacy-and-recency-effects-in-learning/.

"Multiple Intelligences." (n.d.). Identifor. https://www.identifor.com/about/mi.

National Education Association. (n.d.). "Research Spotlight on Homework: NEA Reviews of the Research on Best Practices in Education." National Education Association. http://www.nea.org/tools/16938.htm.

National Geographic. (2016). "Complete Guide to Brain Health." Washington, DC.

National Head Start Association. (n.d.) "About Us: Mission, Vision, History." https://www.nhsa.org/about-us/mission-vision-history.

NSBA. (2009). "National School Boards of America." Alexandria, VA.

Personality Max. (n.d.). "Visual/Spatial Intelligence." https://personalitymax.com/multiple-intelligences/visual-spatial/.

Pinola, M. (2019). "The Science of Memory: Top 10 Proven Techniques to Remember More and Learn Faster." *Zapier*. June 6. https://zapier.com/blog/better-memory/.

Pinto, A. (2018). MS, abstract 122:13.

Ramirez, G., and S. Beilock. (2011). "Writing About Testing Worries Boosts Exam Performance in the Classroom." *Science*, Vol. 331, Issue 6014 (January 14): 211–213.

Read Naturally. (n.d.). "What Is Fluency?" https://www.readnaturally.com/research/5-components-of-reading/fluency.

Renata, R. (2016). *Uses of Classical Conditioning in the Classroom.* San Francisco, CA.

The Research Group. (2017). "Gender Wars." March 21. https://www.researchgrp.com/blog/gender-wars/.

Reimer, J. et al. (1999). *Promoting Moral Growth: From Piaget to Kohlberg.* Long Grove, IL: Waveland Press.

Ruby, M. (2002). "Development: How Math Helps Your Child's Brain Develop." All About Baby. http://www.allaboutbaby.com/infants/mathdevelopment.htm.

Russell, P. (1979). *The Brain Book.* New York: E. P. Dutton.

Rutland, S. D., and Z. Gross. (2017). "Experiential Learning in Informal Educational Settings." *International Review of Education.* Vol. 63, No. 1 (February 2017): 1–8.

Savalia, T. A. Shukla, and R. S. Bapi. (2016). "A Unified Theoretical Framework for Cognitive Sequencing." *Frontiers of Psychology* Vol. 7, No. 1821 (November 18).

Shaywitz, S. E. (2003). *Overcoming Dyslexia: A New and Complete Science-Based Program for Reading Problems at Any Level.* New York: Vintage.

Shiver, E. (2001). "Brain Development and Mastery of Language in the Early Childhood Years." *IDRA Newsletter.* April. https://www.idra.org/resource-center/brain-development-and-mastery-of-language-in-the-early-childhood-years/.

SleepFoundation.org. (n.d.). "Insufficient Sleep among High School Students Associated with a Variety of Health-Risk Behaviors." SleepFoundation.org. https://www.sleepfoundation.org/articles/insufficient-sleep-among-high-school-students-associated-variety-health-risk-behaviors.

Sousa, D. A. (2005). *How the Brain Learns to Read.* Thousand Oaks, CA: Corwin Press.

Stevenson, C. (2002). *Teaching Ten to Fourteen Year Olds* (3rd ed.). Boston, MA: Allyn & Bacon.

Stuart-Squire, L. R., and S. Zola-Morgan. (1988). Memory: Brain systems and behavior. *Trends in Neurosciences, 11*(4) [118], 170–175. http://dx.doi.org/10.1016/0166-2236(88)90144-0. APA. Washington, D.C.

Taylor, K. M., and M. A. Trott. (1991). In Williams, M. S., and S. Shellenberger. (1996). "How Does Your Engine Run?"® A Leader's Guide to the Alert Program® for Self-Regulation. Albuquerque, NM: TherapyWorks, Inc.

Thought Company (2019). New York, NY.

"Tips for Parents: Global vs. Analytic Learners." (2011). The Learning Community. http://www.thelearningcommunity.us/ResourcesbyFormat/TipsforParents/GlobalvsAnalyticLearners/tabid/329/Default.aspx.

Totten Public Schools (2018). Totten, Fort Totten, ND.

Tuckman, B. W., D. A. Abry, and D. R. Smith. (2008). *Learning and Motivation Strategies: Your Guide to Success* (2nd ed.). Upper Saddle River, NJ: Pearson Prentice Hall.

UNICEF Belize. (2014). Facebook update (December 2). https://www.facebook.com/UNICEFBelize/posts/attention-all-parentsa-major-part-of-discipline-is-learning-how-to-talk-with-chi/802840343143947/.

"Understanding Your Learning Style." (n.d.). University of Waterloo. https://uwaterloo.ca/centre-for-teaching-excellence/teaching-resources/teaching-tips/tips-students/self-knowledge/understanding-your-learning-style.

Urban Child Institute (2011). "Data Back 2011 Executive Summary." The Urban Child Institute. Memphis, TN.

Wanamaker, P. (2016). "Sensory Learning Styles." *Milady*. November 21, 2016. https://milady.cengage.com/blog/sensory-learning-styles.

Weimer, M. (2013). "Understanding the Role of Intuition in Teaching." *Faculty Focus*. May 29, 2013. https://www.facultyfocus.com/articles/teaching-careers/understanding-the-role-of-intuition-in-teaching/.

West Sonoma County Public Schools (2019). Public School Attendance Policy. Sebastopol, CA.

Willis, J. (2007). Brain-friendly strategies for the inclusion classroom: Insights from a neurologist and classroom teacher. Indianapolis, IN: Association for Supervision & Curriculum Development.

Women's Brain Health Initiative. (2016). "Packed Daily Schedules Linked to Better Cognitive Function in Old Age." May 18. https://womensbrainhealth.org/great-minds-think-alike/packed-daily-schedule-linked-to-better-cognitive-function-in-old-age.

Wooden, J. (2005). *Game Plan for Life*. London: Bloomsbury Press.

Yopp, H. K. (1992). "Developing Phonemic Awareness in Young Children." *Reading Teacher*, Vol. 45, No. 9: 696–703.

Zimmermann, K. A. (2014). "Procedural Memory: Definition and Examples." Live Science. February 22. https://www.livescience.com/43595-procedural-memory.html.

About the Author

David P. Sortino (Ed.M., Ph.D.) holds a master's degree in human development from Harvard University and a doctorate in clinical psychology from Saybrook University, as well as learning handicapped, resource specialist, and multiple subject teaching credentials. Over the last 40 years he has served as a director to several residential school programs of LH and SED students in public and private education at the elementary, middle, and secondary school levels. He has served as a consultant to state and county programs for at-risk youth (i.e., juvenile hall) and special needs children, and he works directly with individuals and families.

In his private practice, he consults and collaborates with students, parents, teachers, and psychologists to provide support for students' pre-K through college in establishing school success and higher learning levels. He finds that exploring how the brain learns, as well as other learning strategies, can help students develop a better understanding about learning in and out of the classroom. Currently, he directs the Neurofeedback Institute, writes a blog for the *Santa Rosa Press Democrat*, and hosts a bimonthly radio show called *Brain Smart—A Better Learning Brain* on KOWS: 98.7 FM. He is the author of *The Promised Cookie—No Longer Angry Children* (Author House, 2011) and *A Guide to How Your Child Learns—Understanding the Brain from Infancy to Young Adulthood* (Roman & Littlefield, 2017).

www.ingramcontent.com/pod-product-compliance
Lightning Source LLC
Chambersburg PA
CBHW030140240426
43672CB00005B/205